J. Daniel Dodin

E
N
T
E
R

(Reverse Polish Notation Made Easy)

Translated from French by Mary-Denise Dodin
Revised and expanded by Keith Jarett

Published by:
SYNTHETIX
P.O. Box 1080
Berkeley, CA 94701 USA

ISBN 0-9612174-2-1
Library of Congress #84-51380

Also available from SYNTHETIX:

HP-41 Extended Functions Made Easy, by Keith Jarett

HP-41 Synthetic Programming Made Easy, by Keith Jarett

HP-41 Quick Reference Card for Synthetic Programming

French language publications on HP calculators are available from:

Editions du Cagire
77 rue du Cagire
31100 Toulouse FRANCE

FOREWORD

This book is especially for owners of Series 10 HP calculators, including the HP-10C, 11C, 12C, 15C, and 16C. It is designed to help you better understand and utilize your machine. The concepts introduced here apply to all HP calculators, plus a few other calculators that have an ENTER key.

Chapters 1, 2, and 3 will introduce you to how the ENTER key works and how to solve simple problems on your calculator. Chapter 4 introduces the concept of programming. Chapter 5 presents several short application programs, and Chapter 6 gives tips on more efficient use of your Series 10 machine.

ABOUT THE AUTHOR

The author is French. He teaches drafting and engineering calculation at a high school in Toulouse.

He was introduced to Reverse Polish Notation in 1975, with the non-programmable HP-21 calculator. In 1979, when the HP-41C first became available, it was natural for him to order one. Buying a HP-15C when it became available was also somewhat inevitable. He learned about the PPC in early 1981 through Bill Wickes's book "Synthetic Programming on the HP-41C", and in September of the same year founded a PPC chapter in Toulouse. This chapter, with 400 members, was at the time the largest French speaking chapter. The author is also the editor of the French chapter newsletter, PPC-T.

Notation used in this book:

/ denotes division, * denotes multiplication.

Greek letters are avoided, except that pi is written as PI.

The function "square root of x" is written **SQRT**, without any x.

In the programs, the operations are in **boldface** type, preceded and followed by a space.

Digits and other information entered from the keyboard are in normal type. This includes names of variables, which represent numeric data that will be entered from the keyboard.

Examples : sine of 30 degrees is written

30 **SIN** ;

goto 1 is written

GTO 1.

Because prefix keys and displayed codes for program steps vary from one machine to the next, these prefix keys and keycodes will be omitted here.

TABLE OF CONTENTS

INTRODUCTION

Pocket calculators using **Reverse Polish Notation** (RPN for short), featuring the **ENTER** key, have had the reputation among some people of being difficult to understand. Competitive machines that use Algebraic notation (with the = key) claim to be more "natural" to use. Nothing could be further from the truth.

Hewlett-Packard's Series 10 and Series 40 calculators are virtually unique among today's computing devices in their use of RPN. However, some advanced computer languages like FORTH and LISP use the same RPN concept.

As you will see in Chapter 1, RPN and Algebraic notation each have their own logic and special advantages. You will see that in day-to-day calculations RPN is far superior. It's simply a matter of efficiency and ease of use. Examples comparing algebraic and RPN calculations will make this quite clear. If you have an algebraic calculator handy (they are cheap and commonly available), you can follow through the examples both ways and convince yourself.

This book supplements but does not replace the excellent and thorough Owner's Manual supplied with each Hewlett-Packard calculator. A careful reading of the manual, especially after you finish ENTER, is guaranteed to improve your understanding of your machine.

CHAPTER 1

A Matter of Logic

1.1 Language and Logic

A friend of mine, a teacher of mathematics and physics in a French University, pointed out one day that the Chinese have seen their civilization stagnate for centuries, partly on account of a language inconsistent with a high technical level. This may explain why very ancient inventions like the rocket never gave rise to practical developments.

It is said that some Chinese scientists actually think in English. Of course, not all of them do, but the fact that any scientist would choose to think in a foreign language is striking.

Mind is conditioned by language.

As you will see, the "language" of Reverse Polish Notation (RPN) is much better suited to exploratory calculations than is Algebraic Notation. In addition to giving you faster results, RPN may actually improve your ability to think about problems.

1.2 Formulas

Most users of scientific calculators in the western world have acquired a technical and mathematical background from high schools. From France to the United States, these schools use similar mathematical notation.

For example, you probably recognize the formula:

$$x = \frac{-b + (b^2-4ac)^{1/2}}{2a}$$

as the expression for one of the two roots of a quadratic equation.

Here is another example. The figure:

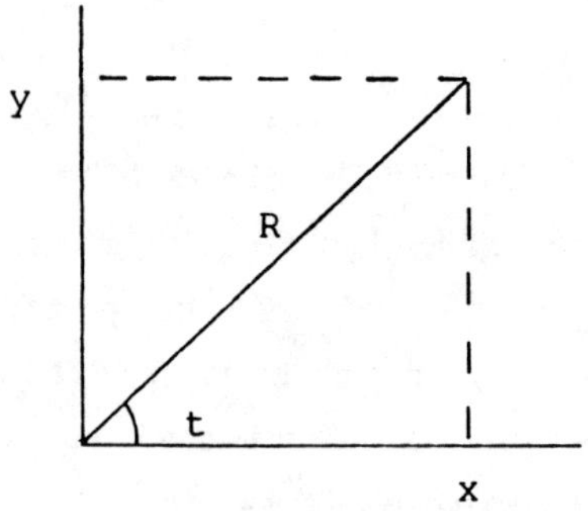

is sufficient for you to realize that R and t are known if x and y are known.

The language of high school mathematics is common to us.

But do you recognize this ?

b **x^2** - a ***** c ***** **4** = **SQRT** - b = **/** **(** **2** ***** a **)** =

or this ?

b **x^2** a **ENTER** c ***** **4** ***** - **SQRT** b - a **/** **2** **/**

I suspect that you recognize neither of them. These are in fact step-by-step procedures to evaluate the preceding mathematical formula. The first procedure applies to algebraic calculators, while the second procedure can be used with machines that use RPN. Details may vary slightly from machine to machine. Boldface letters indicate a key to be pressed. For example, **x^2** means press the **x^2** key.

(On HP Series 10 calculators, you will have to press a shift key, then the key for **x^2**.) The asterisk (*) indicates multiplication. **SQRT** indicates that you should take the square root. Normal (non-boldface) letters mean "key in the value of...", and apply to variables and other inputs to the formula.

This quadratic formula example shows that neither RPN nor algebraic notation is obvious at first.

1.3 Algebraic Notation vs. RPN

To properly appraise the logic underlying the two types of calculator notation, we should compare them with previous operating methods.

The engineer, like the applied mathematician, works essentially with formulas, even though these formulas are often drawn from his memory. He proceeds with his calculations step by step, starting with the known values and calculating intermediate results until the final result is obtained. Problems of the classical form :

unknown quantity = expression (data)

are found more often in textbooks than in actual practice. However, algebraic notation insists that you proceed in this textbook manner. To use this method conveniently and without mistakes, you must write formulas not in their common form but complete with parentheses to indicate the order in which the operations are to be performed. You must also remember to explicitly indicate multiplication where it is implied in the formula.

Most calculators that use algebraic notation have a hierarchy of operations. These operator precedence rules guarantee, for example, that 2+3x4 is interpreted as 2+(3x4), and not as (2+3)x4. These precedence rules cut down on the number of parentheses needed if you can remember the rules and apply them correctly. The need for parentheses can also be partially alleviated by frequent use of the = key. Both of these methods were used in the algebraic notation procedure given on page 8.

In the BASIC computer language, the notation is similar to algebraic calculator notation, except that no = key shortcuts are allowed. For example, the quadratic root formula is written like this:

```
X = (-B+SQR(B↑2-4*A*C))/(2*A)   .
```

Although this resembles the mathematical notation, it is not a "natural" way of working. This type of notation can be justified in computer programming, where complex tasks must be performed. But for simple, day to day calculations, this notation is neither necessary nor convenient. It forces you to think quite far ahead, so that you can open each set of parentheses at the right place.

Reverse Polish Notation, in contrast, allows you to proceed directly to the calculation **without writing a detailed, parenthesized equivalent of the mathematical formula**, and without having to think beyond the next operation. The mathematical formula itself is sufficient to work from. A few examples and a little practice will make this clear.

1.4 Pencil and Paper vs. RPN

To add the numbers 2 and 1 using algebraic notation, you must write down the equation

X = 2 + 1

which is to be performed using the key sequence

2 + 1 = (result).

In contrast, to use Reverse Polish Notation, you should first ask yourself how you would perform this calculation by hand. You find this example unsuitable? Good! This means that you appreciate the ability to take the shortest path to the result!

Certainly you can add 2 and 1 in your head. But suppose you have to add 35728 and 44213? In your head? Of course not! With pencil and paper? Why not? You simply write the two numbers:

35728
44213

and you do the addition. Notice that the nature of the operation is not written down.

It's the same with Reverse Polish Notation. You key in 35728, you get a new line (press **ENTER**), you key in 44213, then you designate the operation to be performed (press +). The result is 79941.

This example illustrates two important characteristics of Reverse Polish notation:

First Principle

Reverse Polish Notation stores numbers. It never stores operations.

Second Principle

Reverse Polish Notation performs operations in the same order in which you would do them by hand.

The first principle reveals the efficiency of RPN. Since there are never any pending (stored) operations, you do not have to keep track of the parentheses in your head. This frees you to concentrate on the structure of the problem, rather than the structure of the calculation.

The second principle reveals that RPN is probably already more familiar to you than you realize. As you use RPN, you will find it more and more natural. Eventually you will wonder how anyone can calculate without it.

CHAPTER 2

Using Reverse Polish Notation (RPN)

2.0 Using RPN

Complete instructions for using RPN can be found in your Owner's Manual. This chapter is intended to be a brief introduction illustrating the power and simplicity of RPN calculation.

2.1 One-number functions

One-number functions, such as **SIN**, **1/x**, and **LOG**, use only the number in the display. They replace that number with the result. For example, to compute the sine of 30 degrees, you would first press

30

to load the number 30 into the display, then

SIN

to calculate the sine. The result is 0.5.

2.2 Two-number functions

When a function, such as + or * (multiplication), requires two numbers, both numbers must be loaded in the calculator <u>before</u> you press the key that executes the function. You use the **ENTER** key to separate the two numbers from each other. For example, to subtract 48 from 722, press

722 **ENTER** 48 - .

The **ENTER** separated the two numbers so you did not get 72,248 when you keyed them in.

2.3 Chain Calculations

Any calculator can do simple calculations involving one or two numbers. When you get to more complex calculations, the advantages of RPN become much more apparent. Chief among these is that intermediate results are displayed as they are calculated, allowing you to check them for reasonableness. Furthermore, intermediate results are handled automatically by the calculator so that they are where you need them when you need them later in the calculation.

As a simple example of a chain calculation, consider the problem (4+5)*(12-7). If you were doing this calculation by hand, you would first evaluate (4+5), then (12-7), then you would multiply the two results. It's the same with RPN. First add 4 and 5:

4 **ENTER** 5 + (result is 9).

Next subtract 7 from 12:

12 **ENTER** 7 - (result is 5).

Now multiply:

* (result is 45).

The order of operations is natural, but you may be wondering how the intermediate result 9 managed to disappear yet still be available for the final multiplication. The next two sections will make this handling of the intermediate results clear.

2.4 The Stack

Intermediate results are stored inside your machine in a group of registers called the **stack**. It is important for you to visualize this stack as you are learning to use RPN. Beginners will also find it helpful to check the contents of the stack (using the roll-down key as explained later) to make sure that the intermediate results are where they should be.

The stack has 4 levels. The bottom register, called X, is always shown in the display. The other registers are named Y, Z, and T (top), as shown here. Each register holds one full-precision number.

```
 _______
|_______|  T
|_______|  Z
|_______|  Y
|_______|  X
```

To see the contents of registers Y, Z, and T, you can rotate the stack downward using the R↓ (roll-down) key, which will be written as **RDN** here. Each press of **RDN** rotates the stack contents down one level, with the displayed number (in X) moving to the top of the stack. To see how this works, load the stack like this:

4 **ENTER** 3 **ENTER** 2 **ENTER** 1

The stack now looks like this:

```
 _______
|___4___|  T
|___3___|  Z
|___2___|  Y
|___1___|  X ,
```

although only the 1 in **X** is visible.

Now consider what happens as you press **RDN** four times:

```
     ___        ___        ___        ___        ___
T   |_4_|      |_1_|      |_2_|      |_3_|      |_4_|   T
Z   |_3_|      |_4_|      |_1_|      |_2_|      |_3_|   Z
Y   |_2_|      |_3_|      |_4_|      |_1_|      |_2_|   Y
X   |_1_|      |_2_|      |_3_|      |_4_|      |_1_|   X
          RDN        RDN        RDN        RDN
```

Each number in the stack is displayed in turn, until the original number returns to the display. At this point the stack is back in its original state.

Tip: pressing **RDN** four times is an easy way to review the contents of the stack without disturbing it.

Another stack manipulation function is **x⇄y**, which will be written here as **X<>Y**. This function exchanges the contents of the X and Y registers. Tip: press **X<>Y** twice if you want to check the contents of the Y register before executing a two-number function. The first **X<>Y** shows you what was in Y, and the second **X<>Y** puts things back where they were.

Some HP calculators, including the HP-11, 15, and 16, have a **R↑** (roll-up) function that rotates the stack upward, with the contents of register T going to X. If you want to rotate the stack upward but you do not have a **R↑** function, press **RDN** three times instead.

The **ENTER** key duplicates the contents of X into Y. The number that was in Y is pushed into Z, and the number that was in Z is pushed into T. (The number that was in T is lost.) After you press **ENTER**, the calculator is prepared to accept a new number which will replace the original copy of the number just **ENTER**ed into Y.

For example, you loaded the stack for the **RDN** example by pressing 4 **ENTER** 3 **ENTER** 2 **ENTER** 1. Each numeric entry went into the X register, and each **ENTER** duplicated the preceding entry in the stack:

T	0	0	0	0	0	4	4	T
Z	0	0	0	4	4	3	3	Z
Y	0	4	4	3	3	2	2	Y
X	4	4	3	3	2	2	1	X
	4	**ENTER**	3	**ENTER**	2	**ENTER**	1	

Note: you may review the stack using **RDN** after a number entry, but not after **ENTER.**

2.5 How the Stack works during calculations

The most important point to remember when using RPN is that the numbers must be in position before you try to perform the operation. For example, to divide 34 by 8, you would first press

34 **ENTER** 8

to load 34 into Y and 8 into X. (Note that for division the position of the numerator in the stack is above the denominator. This is the same as writing a fraction on paper.) Next you would press

÷ (written / here),

the division key, to get the result, 4.25.

The **ENTER** key is not always needed to position a number in the Y register. In fact, the **ENTER** key is only needed when you either have to make a second copy of a number or when you have to separate two numbers that are being entered from the keyboard.

If you have the result of a previous calculation displayed in the X register, that result is <u>automatically</u> pushed up into the Y register when you start to key in a new number. Similarly, the numbers in Y and Z are pushed into Z and T, respectively. When you execute a two-number function, the stack drops automatically. The number that was in Z moves to Y. The number that was in T is duplicated into both T and Z. This automatic lifting and dropping of numbers in the stack is the key to the calculator's efficient and easy-to-use method of handling intermediate results.

An example should make this more clear. Consider the problem (4+5)*(12-7) that you worked earlier. You may want to start with

0 **ENTER ENTER ENTER**

to clear the stack if you plan to use **RDN** to check the stack as you go. In fact, clearing the stack is <u>never</u> necessary prior to starting a calculation unless you are worried that leftover results may confuse you. (They will not confuse the machine.)

Here is a step-by-step trace of the stack contents during the calculation of (4+5)*(12-7):

T										T
Z						9	9			Z
Y		4	4		9	12	12	9		Y
X	4	4	5	9	12	12	7	5	45	X
	4	**ENTER**	5	+	12	**ENTER**	7	-	*	

Registers not shown may contain any previous results or other data. It does not matter since these numbers play no part in the calculation.

In this example, notice that when you keyed in the 12, the previous result 9 was automatically pushed into Y. It remained "floating" just above the 12 until it was needed for the final multiplication. Study this example until you understand it completely.

The concept of intermediate results floating in the stack above current calculations is the essence of the RPN calculation process.

The intermediate results are automatically held in the stack. They are returned to the calculation as needed on a last-in, first-out basis.

Try a few examples on your own to convince yourself that the intermediate results will always be where you need them when you need them in the later stages of the calculation. Here is one more example:

$$\frac{3*(2^7-1)}{(6*7)+(4/12)}$$

The stack is shown horizontally here for convenience. This step-by-step listing is a powerful method for analyzing the usage of the stack.

Function	X	Y	Z	T
2	2			
ENTER	2	2		
7	7	2		
y^x	128			
1	1	128		
-	127			
3	3	127		
*	381			
6	6	381		
ENTER	6	6	381	
7	7	6	381	
*	42	381		
4	4	42	381	
ENTER	4	4	42	381
12	12	4	42	381
/	0.33	42	381	381
+	42.33	381	381	381
/	9.00	381	381	381

All calculators, whether RPN or Algebraic, use a stack. Algebraic machines store each pending operation and the numbers associated with it. With

RPN, there are no pending operations, so only numbers need to be stored in the stack. The other difference is that on Algebraic machines, you have no access to the stack. You just have to hope you put the parentheses in the right places. With RPN, you are in full control at all times.

2.6 The LASTX register

In addition to the four stack registers, your calculator maintains a copy of the number that was in X the last time you executed a numeric function. This copy is kept in a register called the LASTX register. You may be thinking: "What use is this LASTX register? It must not be very important, or I would not have been able to get this far without knowing about it."

While it is true that the LASTX register is not necessary for calculation, it can save you time and frustration. The LASTX register has two uses. First, it can save you from having to re-enter the same number twice. For example, if you are calculating sin(6.24) * tan(6.24/2), you can press

6.24 **SIN** **LASTX** 2 **/** **TAN** ***** .

The LASTX gives you a copy of the number that was in X the last time you executed a function. In this case, it was 6.24 when **SIN** was executed. This number can then be used just as if you had keyed it in by hand.

The second use of LASTX is to correct mistakes. Since we never make mistakes, we can forget this use...

Seriously, suppose you had accidentally pressed the **COS** key instead of the **TAN** key in the last example. You could press

RDN

to get rid of the result cos(6.24/2), then

LASTX

to recover the argument 6.24/2, then

TAN

to complete the correction of the error.

If you press an incorrect two-number function, the recovery procedure is one step longer. For example suppose you want to divide 34 by 8, but you accidentally subtract instead:

34 **ENTER** 8 **-** Whoops!

Now you have 34-8 in **X**. To recover 34 in Y and 8 in X, you must press

LASTX **+**

to undo the subtraction and put 34 in X, then

LASTX

again to put 8 in **X** and push 34 into Y. Now if you press

/ (the ÷ key)

you will get the desired result 34/8 = 4.25.

2.7 Data Storage Registers

Your calculator has several registers that are for your use to save constants, results of earlier calculation, or any other numbers you need to store. These registers are never disturbed by the calculator; they can only be accessed by direct **STO** (store) and **RCL** (recall) commands.

Your Owner's Manual has the details on storage registers for your machine. The principle is simple. If you want to save a value from the display (X-register) in data register number 0, just press

STO 0

If you want to recover a value that you saved earlier in register 5, press

RCL 5

What could be simpler?

If you make frequent or extensive use of data registers, it is a good idea to keep notes of what number is stored where. This can save you a bit of frustration as you search for that number you just stored a few minutes ago.

Since the HP-45, HP calculators have had storage register arithmetic capability. For example, to add 5 to register 3, you would press

5 **STO+3** .

Using the other three arithmetic operations you can subtract a number in X from a register, multiply by a number in X, and divide by a number in X.

The HP-11C, 15C, and 16C have a special index register, designated I. (This is not to be confused with the interest register on the HP-12C, designated i.) The index register is used for advanced features like indirect addressing and loop control. It is accessed just like any other register, by **STO I** and **RCL I.**

2.8 Fancy Functions

Your calculator has some complex functions that mimic similar functions on computers. Their structure is often hybrid, partly algebraic and partly RPN. For example, DSE (Decrement and Skip if Equal), a function which will be covered in section 4.2.6, uses an operand (a register number) that is keyed in after the DSE. This is reminiscent of algebraic logic. However another operand is given before the DSE, because the contents of the register must be prepared before the DSE is executed.

Chapter 4, which introduces the subject of programming, covers this class of functions. If you do little or no programming, you will not need to learn all about these functions, but at least you will get an idea what all those extra functions on your keyboard are good for.

CHAPTER 3

Calculating in Reverse Polish Notation

3.1 Introducing the Hewlett-Packard RPN machines

If you are reading this book, you probably own or have the use of a Hewlett-Packard (HP) calculator. All HP calculators use Reverse Polish notation, except the HP-71B.

The HP's first scientific calculator was, of course, the HP-35, introduced in 1972. Since then, many more models have come and gone: the HP-45, 80, 55, 65, 67, 70, 91, 92, 97, 10 (the handheld printing calculator), 19, 29, 21, 22, 25, 27, 29, 31, 32, 33, 34, 37, and 38. Some of the later models have carried the designation **C**, indicating Continuous Memory. Since these models are no longer available, I will not describe them here. If you have one of them, consult your Owner's Manual for details of its use.

This book is designed primarily for users of the popular new Series 10 calculators. However, users of the HP-41 or of one of the older HP calculators will be able to use the techniques described here with just a few variations.

3.1.1 Series 40

The HP-41C, CV, and CX are very advanced programmable calculators. Their alphanumeric display, keyboard redefinition capability, and advanced programming features provide a wonderful combination of convenience and power.

If you currently own a Series 10 calculator, this book will help you get the most out of your machine. But if you ever decide that you really need something more powerful, take a look at the HP-41.

3.1.2 Series 10

The Series 10 machines are HP's first horizontal format calculators. They differ from their predecessors in two important respects. First they are much thinner, so they can be carried in your pocket without filling it completely. Although details vary from one machine to the next, all the Series 10 calculators share the following features:

The liquid crystal display occupies the upper left portion of the calculator. It is placed slightly to the left to allow room for the batteries.

The numerical keypad is on the right side. It includes the digits from 0 to 9 and the four arithmetic operations.

The function area occupies the left side of the keyboard. Also, because of the shift keys, there are functions associated with the numeric keys as well.

The back side of the machine has a label with some useful information for quick reference.

3.1.3 Special features of each model

HP-10C

As of March 1984, the HP-10C is no longer being manufactured. It was the least expensive Series 10 model, and a successor to the HP-25 and 33. Its programming capability is limited, but it is excellent for day-to-day calculations. Like the other Series 10 machines, it has continuous memory. This means that all the numbers and program instructions in the machine, plus the display setting and other key status information are preserved when you turn the machine off.

HP-11C

This very popular machine is now the least expensive HP calculator available. It is nevertheless quite powerful, with hyperbolic functions, a random number generator, 203 bytes of memory, and the very useful backarrow (digit entry correction) key. The 11C is eminently suitable for students and engineers who are willing to pay for quality and who do not need the advanced features of the HP-15 or HP-41.

Unless you use them, advanced functions merely clutter the keyboard, making the functions that you do use harder to find. The simplest machine that fills your current and projected needs is the best choice.

HP-15C

The most powerful Series 10 machine, the HP-15C has enough functions to upset a mathematics teacher! Root finding, integration, advanced matrix and complex number operations, and lots of memory make this machine well worth the additional cost compared to the 11C. As an example of the power of these functions, you can multiply all the elements of an 8x8 matrix by 7 in under 5 seconds. You can invert the same matrix in 70 seconds.

Most of the HP-15's advanced functions are not even available as built-in functions on the HP-41! If you think you will be able to use these functions, the 15C is a good choice for you.

HP-12C

This is the financial model of the series, suitable for the day-to-day business calculations of bankers, insurance agents, and real estate agents. The HP-12 succeeds earlier financial calculators made by HP, providing essentially the same functions in a much more compact package. The 12C has a modest provision for programming (99 bytes total for data and program). This machine is the only one that uses the BEGIN annunciator which you can see in the display of any Series 10 machine after executing one of the self-test sequences described in the Owner's Manual.

HP-16C

This calculator is designed especially for those people who do a lot of work with computers. Computers typically manipulate numbers in binary (base 2) or hexadecimal (base 16). The HP-16 excels at these manipulations. It can add, subtract, multiply, divide, and much more in four number bases. (Base 8 is thrown in to deal with unusual computer systems, and base 10 is provided for humans.) The HP-16 makes it easy to debug computer programs when, for example, a printout lists the location of the error in hexadecimal. This machine is also a great toy for "bit fiddlers."

3.1.4 Common features, limits

The basic principles of RPN introduced here apply to all HP RPN calculators. Although the examples may be geared to the Series 10 machines, they are easy to adapt to your particular machine. Just consult your Owner's Manual if you are in doubt as to how to do this.

Besides their shape, continuous memory, and Reverse Polish Notation, the Series 10 machines have flexible memory allocation. You can allocate part of the memory as data registers and part as program steps. One register equals 7 program steps (except on the HP-16C, where registers can be different sizes). In effect, you can trade a few data registers for more program space, or vice versa. The amount of program steps in memory determines the program allocation; everything left over is available as data registers (including matrix and complex stack data on the HP-15C). So don't be misled by the 448 program steps advertised for the HP-15C. First consider the impracticality of keying in such a long program. Second, you will need quite a few data registers to be able to use the advanced matrix operations.

Now a few points of operating philosophy. The Series 10 machines are handheld calculators designed first and foremost to perform manual calculations quickly and efficiently, and **incidentally** to run a program. Programs are simply a means of customizing your calculator by adding supplementary and specific functions.

The Series 10 machines cannot be compared with BASIC microcomputers, because BASIC machines are very poor tools for manual calculations. They are instead designed primarily to run programs, and they succeed very well in that respect. This difference between RPN and BASIC machines permeates all the architectural and operational aspects of the machines. The keyboard layout of an RPN machine has function keys that allow you to execute functions with a very few keystrokes. BASIC machines require you to spell out the name of each function you use. (The HP-41 is an intermediate case in which only the frequently used functions are directly available on the keyboard.) Program organization and execution differs greatly between the two types of machines, as well.

With the Series 10 you have a very smooth, tactile feedback keyboard which relieves you of the need to check the display as you press the keys. There is, however, no alphabetic display capability.

The main disadvantages of programming on the Series 10 machines are that the program length is limited and the program execution is slow. The main advantages are that there is no programming language to learn, and that for simple problems you can often get a result faster than you could, for example, using BASIC.

3.2 How to approach a calculation

3.2.1 Formulas

Suppose you wish to evaluate the quadratic formula

$$x = \frac{-b + (b^2-4ac)^{1/2}}{2a} \quad ,$$

where the values of **a**, **b**, and c are known.

There are two possible ways to evaluate this formula. The "brute force" approach is to proceed from left to right. A more natural approach is to work the problem starting from the inside and working outward.

Here's how the "brute force" approach works in

RPN:

b CHS ENTER x^2 4 **ENTER** a * c * -
SQRT + 2 **ENTER** a * /

For example: a=-1, b=2, c=3 gives x=-1. This keystroke sequence makes use of one trick: after the first **ENTER**, you don't have to re-enter the value of b. The value -b is already in the display, and $(-b)^2$ is the same as b^2. Now let's look at the status of the stack during the calculation.

Function	LASTX	X	Y	Z	T
b	-	b	-	-	-
CHS	-	-b	-	-	-
ENTER	-	-b	-b	-	-
x^2	-b	b^2	-b	-	-
4	-b	4	b^2	-b	-
ENTER	-b	4	4	b^2	-b
a	-b	a	4	b^2	-b
*	a	4a	b^2	-b	-b
c	a	c	4a	b^2	-b
*	c	4ac	b^2	-b	-b
-	4ac	b^2-4ac	-b	-b	-b
SQRT	b^2-4ac	R	-b	-b	-b
+	R	-b+R	-b	-b	-b
2	R	2	-b+R	-b	-b
ENTER	R	2	2	-b+R	-b
a	R	a	2	-b+R	-b
*	a	2a	-b+R	-b	-b
/	2a	-b+R/2a	-b	-b	-b

Abbreviations used:

- = don't care

R = $(b^2-4ac)^{1/2}$

Because all 4 levels of the stack are used, the value -b is duplicated from register T as the stack drops. This causes -b to be left in stack registers T, Z, and Y at the completion of the calculations. With a more complicated formula, you could easily exhaust the capabilities of the 4-level stack if you attempted to proceed directly from left to right. Unless you were very careful not to push data off the top of the stack, your result would be incorrect.

This illustrates a danger of the left-to-right method. Besides being dangerous and difficult to follow, this left-to-right method is inefficient.

Let's look at the inside-out method:

4 **ENTER** a * c * **CHS** b $\mathbf{x^2}$ + **SQRT** b - 2 / a /

This is only one step shorter than the left-to-right solution, but if you investigate the stack usage, you will see that only the X and Y registers are used. This makes the process easier to follow. In fact, this is by far a more natural way to proceed. **Each value is keyed in only when it will be used immediately for a calculation.** This is exactly the way you would proceed when doing a pencil-and-paper calculation. The last few steps of this keystroke sequence illustrate another helpful technique. The multiplication in the denominator is performed as a sequence of divisions, rather than a multiplication followed by a division. This avoids raising the stack.

The real power of the inside-out calculation method is the speed with which it can be used "on the fly", when you perform calculations without writing equations.

3.2.2 Calculating "on the fly"

Suppose you want to calculate how far away a satellite is when it is 5 degrees above the horizon as seen from an earth station. You know the radius of the earth is

$$r_e = 6378 \text{ kilometers.}$$

For this example, assume that the satellite is in a circular orbit at an altitude of

$$h = 800 \text{ kilometers.}$$

The figure below shows the triangle formed by the center of the earth, the satellite, and the earth station's location on the earth's surface. The line from the earth station to the satellite is 5 degrees above a tangent, so that the satellite appears 5 degrees above the horizon.

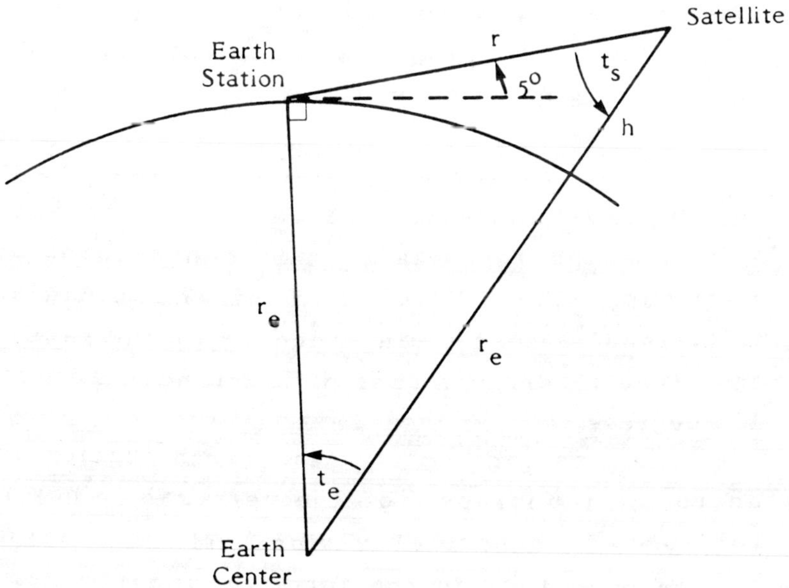

It is clear from the figure that enough information has been given to compute the range r from the earth station to the satellite. However, as is typically the case in real problems, the formula needed to compute the result is not simple.

There are at least two ways to proceed. The simpler way is to use the law of sines:

$$\frac{a}{\sin A} = \frac{b}{\sin B} = \frac{c}{\sin C},$$

where a, b, and c are the three sides of a triangle and A, B, and C are the angles opposite sides a, b, and c, respectively. If you were to spend a minute or two with pencil and paper, you could probably come up with the formula:

$$r = (r_e+h)\sin(180-95-\sin^{-1}(r_e(\sin\ 95)/(r_e+h)))/\sin\ 95.$$

With an RPN calculator, you don't have to work this way. Instead, you proceed step-by-step toward the solution using nothing more than the law of sines formula. You save several minutes even before you start!

To get the value of r, you will need to know the opposite angle (at the center of the earth). You can find the size of this central angle by first computing the size of the other two angles in the triangle, then taking account of the fact that the three interior angles of a triangle add up to 180 degrees.

The interior angle at the earth station is 95 degrees, 90 degrees from the vertical to horizontal, plus 5 degrees elevation. The law of sines can be used to find the interior angle t_s at the satellite:

$$(r_e+h)/\sin 95 = r_e/\sin t_s, \text{ or}$$
$$t_s = \sin^{-1}(\ r_e/((r_e+h)/\sin 95)\ )$$

The value of the ratio $(r_e+h)/\sin 95$ will be needed to apply the law of sines after you have computed the earth-center angle, so you should store it in a data register. The keystroke sequence is

6378 **ENTER** 800 **+** 95 **SIN** **/** **STO 1**

6378 **X<>Y** **/** **SIN^{-1}**

The result is 62.3 degrees. Next, compute the earth-center angle

$$t_c = 180 - 95 - t_s$$

The keystroke sequence, with t_s still in the display, is

180 **X<>Y** **-** 95 **-**

The result is 22.7 degrees. Now, to get the range to the satellite, note that the law of sines gives

$$r/\sin t_c = (r_e+h)/\sin 95, \text{ or}$$
$$r = (\sin t_c)*(r_e+h)/\sin 95$$

The keystroke sequence, with t_c in the display and $(r_e+h)/\sin 95$ in register 1 is

SIN **RCL 1** *****

The result is 2784 kilometers. The most striking feature of the RPN solution to this real problem is that no elaborate manipulation of equations was required. You simply proceeded one step at a time, using formulas simple enough that you really didn't even need to write them down.

In addition to helping you avoid detailed equations, this procedure gives you more confidence in the result. You get to see and check the intermediate results, rather than having the whole thing evaluated at once when you press an = key.

3.3 Advanced uses

Is it necessary to know how to perform very long calculations on these machines? Not if you don't want to. Any long calculation consists of a series of shorter calculations. If you were using pencil and paper, you would do each calculation, writing down the results. Then you would use these intermediate results to compute the final result.

It's the same with RPN calculators. You can compute each intermediate result and use the STO (store) function to put the result in one of the calculator's data registers. Whenever you need that intermediate result, RCL (recall) brings it back from storage. In addition to using the calculator's storage, it is a good idea to write down the first few digits of each intermediate result in case you forget which register you used to store a particular intermediate result. Remember, a calculator does not completely replace your pencil and paper. It merely provides faster, more accurate results.

Remember when using pencil and paper as a memory aid that the calculator's data registers contain the full-precision intermediate results. The display setting (FIX 2, for example), rounds the displayed value, but not the internal value. **For maximum accuracy, approximate on the final result, and on the final result only. Do not round or re-key any of the intermediate results.**

If you make a mistake during a calculation, you should either use the LASTX capability to correct the mistake (if you can do so carefully enough to avoid altering stack registers Z and T), or you should redo the calculation from the beginning. If the calculation is important, you should probably do it a second time as a check anyway.

When you are doing long calculations, it is impractical to start over after a mistake. The simple solution is to break the calculation into several parts. Write down and store the exact results from each part, so that you will never need to redo more than one portion of the calculation.

Another solution to the problem of long calculations is to write a program to perform the calculation. This is the best approach if you will have to do the same calculation more than a few times.

CHAPTER 4

Reverse Polish Notation programming

4.0 Keystroke sequence or program?

The Owner's Manuals all explain that a program is merely the same series of keystrokes that you would use to solve the problem by hand. When you run a program, the calculator executes the same internal ("microcode") instructions that it would have executed if you performed the calculation one keystroke at a time. There are, nevertheless, three differences. These are: memory usage, flow control instructions, and preparation time.

4.1 First difference: Memory Usage

You saw in the last example of Chapter 3 that it is often necessary to use the same value twice in a calculation. The simple solution is to store the value in a data register for later use.

If you use more than two memories, it starts to get difficult to remember which value was stored where. With a program, the program's development (figuring out the correct keystroke sequence) is separate from its utilization. This makes it much more practical to write down on a piece of paper the role of each data register. For example (R means register):

R_0 = radius of the earth
R_1 = orbit altitude
R_2 = elevation angle

When you are doing a calculation manually, it is most convenient to key in each number as it is needed. However when you utilize a program, it is more convenient to key in all the data before starting the program, so that the program does not have to halt to let you key in more data. For this purpose, the RPN stack is invaluable. For example, if you were utilizing a program to compute the distance to a satellite, you might want it to be usable by pressing

earth radius **ENTER** orbit altitude
ENTER elevation angle

to load the necessary data into the stack. The order in which you enter the numbers is important, because the program can only identify each number by its position is the stack. If this is a concern, you can construct the program so that the initialization for each usage is done with data registers. For example,

earth radius **STO 0** orbit altitude **STO 1**
elevation angle **STO 2** .

This is the only way you can initialize a multi-input program on a non-RPN machine, and some people feel more comfortable working this way. However the **ENTER** method of initializing the program saves one keystroke per entry, and is the approach most often used by experienced RPN programmers.

Once you have all the data in the stack, you can review it by pressing the roll-down key 4 times before starting the program. The **X<>Y** key or **R↑** key (if available) can also be used to review the stack. Be sure to put the stack back in its original configuration before you start the program!

Depending on its complexity, the program can use the data directly from the stack or store it in data registers first, using a sequence like

LBL A (allows you to start the program by pressing the **A** key.)
STO 2 Store the elevation angle.
RDN Roll down the stack.

STO 1 Store the orbit altitude.

RDN Roll down the stack.

STO 0 Store the earth radius.

Sequences like this are commonly found at the beginning of programs. Their only purpose is to simplify the use of the program.

4.2 Flow control instructions

Flow control instructions, which have no use except in programs, include labels, stops, branches, tests, and counting instructions.

The **P/R** (program/run) key allows you to enter and leave program mode. When you switch into program mode, the calculator displays one line of the program. This position in the program is simply the location where the machine stopped the last time the program was run. The calculator keeps a record of this position in continuous memory. The internal register in which this position is kept is called the **program pointer** register. You can visualize the program pointer as an arrow pointed at the current line of a program, that is, the line that will be executed next.

Because the display lacks alphabetic characters, each line is represented by a numeric code. Each two-digit number of this code represents one keystroke. The first digit is the row number of the key, and the second digit is the column number (0 indicates the tenth column on the Series 10 machines). Decimal digits are shown shown by their own values, 0 through 9 (one digit only).

While in program mode, any keys that you press will be inserted into the program following the line in the display. The program can be reviewed one step at a time by pressing the **SST** (single-step) key, or continuously if you hold the key. The **BST** (back-step) key allows you to go backwards. Line 000 is a place-holder at the top of the program. It is needed to allow you to insert new instructions in front of the first instruction in the program.

4.2.1 Labels

Label instructions (**LBL n**) on the HP-11, 15, and 16 allow you to mark positions in a program, so that you can quickly get to the start of important sections of the program. Alphabetic labels like **LBL A** permit single-key execution of sections of your program. See your Owner's Manual for details. The number of available labels varies with the power of the calculator, but you should find the number quite reasonable compared to the maximum program size that the calculator allows.

On the HP-10 and 12, no labels are provided because of the limited program size. (Each label uses one program line.) Instead of using labels on these machines, you must refer to positions in the program by line number.

4.2.2 Run/Stop

The Run/Stop function (**R/S**) stops a running program. If the program is not running, **R/S** will start it running at the current line.

The **SST** (single-step) and **BST** (back-step) keys allow you to review the program one step at a time in program mode. In run mode, the **SST** key allows you to execute the program one step at a time. If you hold down the **SST** key, the current line of the program will be displayed. The instruction is executed when you release the **SST** key. (On the HP-15 in matrix mode, and on the HP-41, you can abort the execution of the line by holding the key.)

The **PSE** (pause) instruction stops the program for a second or so, displaying the contents of the X register.

4.2.3 Branching

The **GTO** (go to), **GSB** (go subroutine), and **RTN** (return) instructions allow you to jump to any location in the program.

GTO, followed by a label name (on the HP-11, 15, or 16) or a line number (on the HP-10 or 12), jumps the program pointer to the designated label or line. This works the same from the keyboard or in a running program.

GSB, followed by a label name or line number, works differently from the keyboard than it does in a running program. From the keyboard, it starts running the program at the designated label or line. In a running program, it inserts the execution of the named subroutine in the main program. For alphabetic labels, the **GSB** can sometimes be omitted. See your manual for details.

4.2.4 Test Instructions

One of the most powerful features that you can put in a program is conditional execution. Depending on the outcome of a certain test, different segments of the program can be executed. This allows you to apply a different formula over different intervals of variable values:

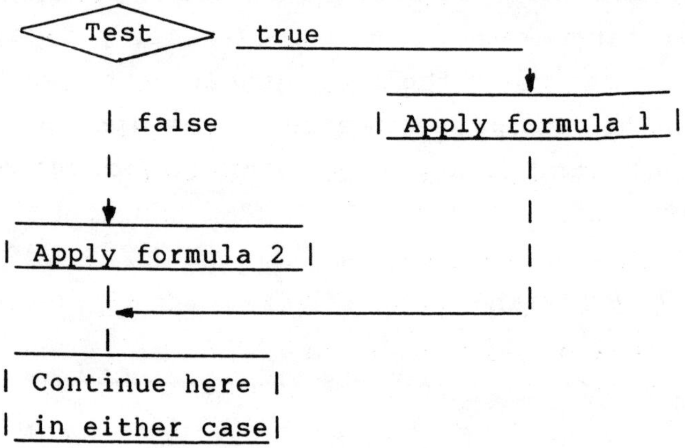

On the HP-11C, the test instructions X≤Y, X>Y, X≠Y, X=Y, X<0, X>0, X≠0, and X=0 are available. The other Series 10 machines have similar test instructions. Twelve tests are available on the HP-15. The test instruction causes the following line to be executed if the test is true, and skipped otherwise. Usually the line following the test instruction is a **GTO** instruction. For example:

Instruction	Effect
...	
...	
X=0	If x=0,
<-- **GTO 9**	then skip to **LBL 9**.
| ...	Otherwise ignore the **GTO**
| ...	and continue with this
| ...	block of instructions.
| ...	
--> **LBL 9**	(This would be line 09 on the HP-10C or 12C, since they do not use labels.)

Suppose you were trying to write a program to compute the complex roots of any quadratic equation. Depending on whether b^2-4ac is positive, you have to apply different formulas. Without the conditional execution capability that test instructions give you, your task would be terribly complicated.

If your problem has the structure shown in the following flowchart, it is convenient to use a **GSB** instruction instead of a **GTO** following the test.

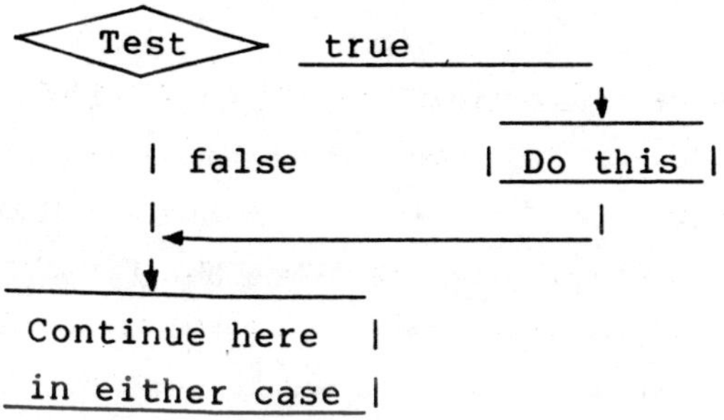

An even greater simplification is possible if you only need to conditionally execute a single instruction. Then instead of using a **GSB** instruction, you can substitute the actual single instruction you want to execute if the test is true. For example, suppose you want a program to treat all negative inputs as zero. The sequence

X<0	If x is negative,
CLX	then substitute zero.

placed at the beginning of the program, will do the job. (On the HP-15, use **TEST2** for **X<0.**)

Tests can sometimes be used in even more clever ways. For example, the sequence

```
X=0
1
.
```

enters the value 1.0 if x is zero, 0 if x is not zero. The sequence

```
X>Y
1/x
*
```

performs division if x is greater than y, multiplication otherwise.

Tests for equality should be used with care. The problem is that values which should be equal are sometimes very slightly different due to rounding errors. For example, if you compute the **SIN** of PI in radian mode, you will find that the result is -4.1×10^{-10}. Of course the expected answer is zero. But in fact the PI that your calculator uses only represents the first 10 digits of PI.

If you are working with values that may contain roundoff error, do not demand strict equality. Instead, round the numbers first if your calculator has a **RND** (round) function, or use an inequality test. For instance, in the sine of pi example, you could test whether the absolute value of x is less than 10^{-8}. These cautions against demanding exact equality apply even more strongly to a test used to control a loop. For example if you use the sequence

```
LBL A
...
...
X≠0
GTO A   ,
```

an "infinite loop" will occur if x does not become exactly zero.

4.2.5 Flags (HP-11C, 15C, and 16C only)

A flag is a yes/no indicator that can be initialized either by you or by the status of the calculator. The "yes" and "no" states of the flag are referred to as "set" and "clear", respectively.

Flag 8 on the HP-15C is an example of a status flag. Whenever you perform a complex number operation, the calculator sets flag 8 and lights up the "C" annunciator in the display. This indicates that the complex number mode is active. Similarly, if you use **SF 8** to set flag 8 directly, the complex number mode and annunciator are also activated. The instruction **CF 8** (clear flag 8) de-activates the complex number mode.

Other HP machines have different numbers of flags. The HP-41 has 56. Flags may be set (**SF n**), cleared (**CF n**), or tested (**F? n**), where **n** is the number of the flag.

The most important use of flags is to allow delayed conditional execution. For example, suppose you want the program to subtract 2 from X if x is greater than y. The difficulty is that the X and Y registers are not set up properly for subtracting 2 at the time the comparison of x and y is made. This problem can be easily overcome by using a flag:

SF 0	Make sure that flag 0 is set to start.
X>Y	If X is greater than Y,
CF 0	then clear flag 0. Otherwise flag 0 stays set.

```
2
F? 0          If flag 0 is set,
CLX           change the 2 to zero.
-             Subtract 2 if X was greater
               than Y, zero otherwise.
```

Flags can also provide mode selections for your programs. For example, you can use a flag to control whether intermediate results are displayed:

```
F? 1          If flag 1 is set,
PSE           then pause and display X.
...           Otherwise do not pause.
```

4.2.6 Counting instructions

4.2.6.1 ISG and DSE

The most powerful conditional execution instructions on Hewlett-Packard calculators, including the Series 10 machines, are the loop control instructions. You have already seen how to construct a loop using a label at the top of the loop (except the 10C and 12C), and a test instruction followed by a **GTO** at the bottom of the loop. If you use a counter to control the loop, you can subtract 1 from the value of the counter each time through the loop, and continue until it reaches zero:

```
    14        Execute the loop 14 times.
    STO 1     Store initial counter value.
--> LBL 0     Top of loop
|   ...
|   ...       Main body of instructions
|   ...       in the loop
```

```
   |    ...
   |    RCL 1      Recall the counter,
   |    1          subtract 1,
   |    -
   |    STO 1      and store the new value.
   |    X>0        Until the counter becomes zero
   <--  GTO 0      continue the loop.
```

The **ISG** (Increment and Skip if Greater) and **DSE** (Decrement and Skip if Equal) instructions provide a much more compact way of implementing this type of looping. In fact, the preceding example reduces to this simple sequence:

```
        14         Execute loop 14 times.
        STO I      Store initial counter value
                    in the index register.
   -->  LBL 0      Top of loop
   |    ...
   |    ...        Main body of instructions
   |    ...        in the loop
   |    ...
   |    DSE        Decrement and skip if zero;
   <--  GTO 0      otherwise continue the loop.
```

If you are using an HP-15C, use **DSE I** in place of **DSE**. On the HP-11C, the **ISG** and **DSE** instructions do not need a register number, because the index register "I" is always used.

The counter used by the **ISG** and **DSE** instructions has the form **nnnnn.xxxyy**, where **nnnnn** is the current value of the counter, **xxx** is the limit value, and **yy** is the increment. If the increment **yy** is zero, the default value of 1 is assumed. When the calculator encounters an **ISG** instruction in a program, it adds **yy** to **nnnnn**. If the new value of **nnnnn** is greater than **xxx**, the next instruction (usually a **GTO**) is skipped.

DSE works similarly, except that **yy** is subtracted from **nnnnn**, and the next instruction is skipped if the new value of **nnnnn** is equal to or less than **xxx**.

On some HP calculators, including the HP-16C, the **ISG** and **DSE** instructions are replaced by the simpler **ISZ** (increment and skip if zero) and **DSZ** (decrement and skip if zero) instructions. These work similarly to **ISG** and **DSE**. The **xxx** and **yy** fields are ignored. **ISZ** adds one to the number in the index register and skips if the result is exactly zero. **DSZ** subtracts one and skips if the result is zero.

When you want to use the value of a counter within the loop, be sure to strip off the **xxxyy** portion by following the **RCL** instruction with an **INT** instruction.

4.2.6.2 Plain counting

When you want to execute a loop 10 times, you can use the **DSE** (or **DSZ**) instruction as shown in the example on page 53. The sequence is

10 Execute the loop 10 times.
STO I
LBL 0
[instructions to be performed 10 times]
DSE (use **DSE I** on the HP-15)
GTO 0
[remainder of the program].

The counter value in register I starts at **nnnnn**=10. The limit value **xxx** is zero, and the increment **yy** is 1 (the default value).

Each time through the loop, the counter value is reduced by 1 (decremented) and the **GTO 0** instruction sends the pointer back to the top of the loop (**LBL 0**). The counter value becomes 9, then 8, 7, 6, 5, 4, 3, 2, and 1. The tenth time through the loop, the counter value is decremented for the tenth time, from 1 to 0. Since the "equal" condition (**nnnnn=xxx**) is now satisfied, the **GTO 0** instruction is skipped and execution continues through the rest of the program.

If a premature ending of the loop is needed, a good solution can be **1 STO I.** This sets the counter to 1, so that the **GTO 0** instruction at the bottom of the loop will be skipped. Note that **CLX** will work as well as **1** with **DSE,** but not with **DSZ.**

Some programs may require a variable number of loop executions according to the internal conditions in the loop. You can use **STO I** to change the counter as needed. Sorting programs usually need this kind of approach. It gets a little tricky sometimes, but it can be done.

4.2.6.3 Counting between two values

In this case the loop is to be repeated a certain number of times, but the counter must take values different from the loop number. The counter register has to be initialized with **xxx** as well as **nnnnn** fields. The **yy** field is only needed if an increment other than 1 is desired. Note also that the **ISZ** and **DSZ** functions provided on some HP calculators do not allow this type of looping to be implemented directly.

For example, to count from 10 to 15, you would use a sequence like this:

```
        10.015     Start at 10, stop at 15.
        STO I      Store initial counter value.
    --> LBL 0      Top of loop
   |    ...
   |    ...        Main body of instructions
   |    ...        in the loop
   |    ...
   |    ISG        Increment and skip if >15;
    <-- GTO 0      otherwise continue the loop.
```

It is usually a matter of programming convenience whether you use **ISG**, counting forward, or **DSE**, counting backward.

As another example, suppose you want to count from 100 down to 50 by 5. You would use **DSE** with an initial counter value of 100.04505. The "equal" condition is set to 45, so that the loop will still be executed once more after the counter reaches 50. To count up from 50 to 100 by 5, use **ISG** and an initial counter value of 50.10005.

When the **nnnnn** or **xxx** value is the result of a previous calculation, you should be aware of the fact that the instructions in the loop will be executed once even if the final value has already been passed. If this is a concern, you can test the counter value with an **ISG** or **DSE** instruction before entering the loop. Another alternative is to use a structure like this:

```
LBL A      Top of loop.
ISG        If final value is not reached,
GTO B      then jump to LBL B section.
GTO C      Else skip to rest of program.
```

```
LBL B      [Instructions to be executed
...        each time through the loop]
GTO A      Return to top of the loop.
LBL C      [Remainder of the program]
```

This double-**GTO** structure accomplishes the equivalent of a "increment and skip if not greater" instruction. There is a slightly less cumbersome approach that gives the same result. For this technique, you need to follow the **ISG** or **DSE** instruction with a test instruction that will always give a FALSE condition. For example, if the X register is known to contain a positive number, you can use the sequence:

```
LBL A      Top of loop.
ISG        If final value is not reached,
X<0        then skip over the GTO C.
GTO C      Else skip to rest of program.
...        [Instructions to be executed
...        each time through the loop]
GTO A      Return to top of the loop.
LBL C      [Remainder of the program]
```

It may be more convenient to use a flag test for the "skip" instruction (**X<0** here). Any test that can be guaranteed to yield a FALSE condition will do the job.

4.2.6.4 Negative numbers

The **ISG** and **DSE** instructions have one deficiency: the limit value **xxx** cannot be negative. You can count from -50 to 100, but not from 100 to -50.

The simplest way around this problem is to

count from -100 to 50 and to use the sequence **INT, CHS** before using the counter in a calculation. However if the counting limits are calculated within the program and are not known beforehand, solving the problem of a negative limit is much more difficult. In this situation, it may be best to abandon the **ISG** and **DSE** instructions and use other methods of loop control.

You will face similar problems if you need a limit value greater than 999 or an increment greater than 99. Fortunately, these constraints on **ISG** and **DSE** are rarely a problem in normal programming.

If you ever do need to construct your own counter, use the loop control technique illustrated in section 4.2.6.1.

4.3 Constructing a program

There are several types of programs that are appropriate for a calculator. First are the "disposable" programs -- those that will be used only once. These are usually very simple, short routines that do not use looping or other advanced features. They can be written immediately at the keyboard. They are typically used to perform the same operation on many different pieces of data.

Second are general-purpose programs that you will use more than once. These are usually written down on paper so that they can be quickly keyed in when needed.

Finally, don't forget the demonstration programs intended to impress your friends (provided that you don't tell how many hours you spent developing them). Chapter 5 contains some programs of this sort.

4.3.1 Instant programs

You will often need short programs to perform the same calculation several times. The program is a sequence of steps identical to the steps that would be used to perform the calculation by hand. No looping or testing is involved.

Here is a typical example. Recently some fellow teachers and I were correcting 600 copies of an examination. Each score consisted of three parts which totaled to 80 points for a perfect score. Since the normalized score was to be a number from 0 to 20, we needed to add the three score components and divide by 4.

This task is certainly not difficult, but when you are doing it 600 times you should invest a little time to speed up the process. A simple program does the job:

+ + R/S 4 /

To use this program, take the three components of the score (call them a, b, and c) and load them in the stack:

a **ENTER** b **ENTER** c .

Then a press of

R/S

provides the raw score out of 80. Another press of

R/S

provides the normalized score out of 20. Any fractional part is rounded up to the next integer, but this is most quickly done mentally.

This example shows how, with a bare minimum of programming effort, you can save yourself significant amounts of time in simple, repetitive calculations.

One note: pressing R/S to start this program assumes that you are at the top of the program to begin with. Before you use the program for the first time, you should press

RTN

in run (non-program) mode to set the program pointer to the top of the program (line 000). After each time you use the program, the / instruction will leave the pointer at line 000 again. If you want this program to co-exist with other programs in the calculator, you will have to add a **RTN** instruction to get the pointer to line 000 after the / instruction (see section 6.17).

Even for short programs like this, it makes sense to write the program down on paper and to test it once using **SST**. But for the quickest results, avoid trying any fancy stuff. Using the stack for inputs and results is highly recommended, because it simplifies the usage of the program. Then, as long as there are no more than 4 inputs and 4 results, you won't have to stop the program.

4.3.2 More elaborate programs

Now let's consider the quadratic equation example from Chapter 3. It may not be the most useful example, but it should at least be familiar to you. From the calculation example of section 3.2.1, we can write a simple program:

LBL A 4 ENTER R/S STO 2 * R/S * CHS
R/S STO 1 x^2 + SQRT RCL 1 2 / RCL 2 /

Notice that we have substituted **R/S** for the letters a, b, and c. At each **R/S** instruction, the program stops so that you can key in the appropriate value (a, then c, then b). After keying in each value, you have to press **R/S** to restart the program. The **STO** and **RCL** instructions have been introduced to avoid the need to re-enter the same data.

Running this program is a fairly tedious undertaking. First you press **GSB A** to get the program started. Then the program stops for you to key in the value of a (-1 in the example from Chapter 3, so press 1 **CHS**). You press **R/S** to restart the program, and it stops again for you to input the value of c (3 in this example). Another press of **R/S** and the calculator stops again for the value of b (2 here). Press **R/S** again and the result finally appears: -1.

This method of programming, while it is very much like what non-RPN calculators force you to do, is not usually necessary on RPN calculators. The order of data entry is not natural, errors during data entry can disrupt the calculation, and the continual starting and stopping is annoying.

Let's try to rewrite this program assuming that the user of the program will introduce all the data at the beginning, using the very reasonable sequence:

a **ENTER** b **ENTER** c

This makes the programming job a little more difficult because now the data has to be extracted from the stack. But you only have to write the program once; you have to use it a great number of times. Therefore it makes a lot of sense to make the program easy to use.

At the beginning of the program the stack will contain c in X, b in Y, and a in Z. The value c is used only once (to compute 4ac), so it doesn't make sense to store c in a register. A reasonable first operation for the program is then to roll down the stack to get to the value **b**, which needs to be stored for later use. Since b^2 is needed before b, an x^2 instruction is appropriate here. So far we have the steps

RDN STO 1 x^2,

after which the stack contains:

T = c

Z = don't care

Y = a

X = b^2

LASTX = b

and

R1 = b

Next we need to save the value of a and subtract 4ac from b^2. This is easy to do with these steps:

X<>Y STO 2 R↑ * 4 * - .

The **R↑** brings the value of c back into the X register. On machines without a **R↑** (roll-up) function, you can use three roll-downs instead.

The registers now contain:

T = don't care

Z = don't care

Y = don't care

X = b^2-4ac

LASTX = 4ac

and

R1 = b

R2 = a .

Now the calculation is easy to complete:

SQRT RCL 1 - 2 / RCL 2 /

(square root, subtract b, divide by 2a). The result is left in the X register.

Here is the complete program:

LBL A RDN STO 1 x^2 X<>Y STO 2 R↑ *

4 * - SQRT RCL 1 - 2 / RCL 2 /

The length of this program is essentially the same as the previous monstrosity, but it's far easier to use. Just press

a ENTER b ENTER c GSB A

and you get the result.

Sure, it's a little extra effort to program this way, but if you plan to use the program a lot (and you shouldn't be writing programs if this isn't the case), you will save time and frustration in the long run. Just keep this simple principle in mind:

All the data should be in the stack at the start of the program.

If there are more than 4 inputs (your problem may already be too complex for a calculator), input just the first four. Let the program perform any reductions and data storage necessary to free the stack. The program can then halt for input of the next 4 values.

When a program has two or more results, it is good programming practice to put the primary result in X, the secondary result in Y, and so forth. This way it is easy to review the results as many times as you want without having to restart the program. If the program calculates only one result at a time, using **R/S** to start the calculation of each secondary result, earlier results may be lost. This means that you will have to restart the program to get another look at earlier results.

Now let me dispel a popular myth. It is not generally true that programming "tricks" will produce great improvements in a program. You will save a few steps here and there, but you are unlikely to significantly shorten the program unless you rethink the structure of the algorithm behind the program.

The preceding program is a good example of this. You can use clever tricks to shorten it a little bit, but this is probably not worth your time to do.

As another example, let's extend the quadratic solution program to make it more generally useful. This time, we will allow for both roots of the equation and also allow for the case in which the roots are complex numbers.

The complete formula is:

$$\frac{-b \pm (b^2-4ac)^{1/2}}{2a}$$

Using a little algebra you can incorporate the division into the numerator:

$$-(b/2a) \quad \pm \quad [(b/2a)^2-(c/a)]^{1/2}$$

In this form it is easy to see that the calculation can be simplified. Rather than dealing directly with a, b, and c, you can first compute b/2a and c/a, after which it is easy to get the result. This simplification of the problem by manipulating the formula is the most important step in developing an efficient program.

Now you are ready to write the program to evaluate the formula. You can start by writing the sequence of instructions that you would use to do the computation directly on the keyboard. Wherever you need a value that you have used before, you should review the program to see whether you can keep a copy of the value in the stack.

To duplicate a value in the stack, you can use **ENTER**. You should be aware that **ENTER** temporarily disables the automatic stack lift. If the **ENTER** is followed by a **RCL** or any similar instruction that loads a number into the X register, the duplicated value in the X register will be overwritten. In this situation, the **ENTER** has no effect. You can overcome this problem by using two **ENTER**s or by rearranging the program so that the **ENTER** is followed by a stack or arithmetic operation. [On the HP-41, you can use **RCL X** to duplicate the value in X without disabling the stack lift. Since this book primarily concerns Series 10 machines, such advanced capabilities are not assumed.] For more details on stack lift, consult your Owner's Manual.

If you are out of stack registers or if you prefer not to juggle numbers within the stack, you can use a **STO** instruction to create a copy of a value that you will need later. Purists like to create programs that only use the stack, so that the storage registers are not disturbed. Often these programs are shorter and faster than versions which use data registers.

There are two disadvantages of programs that juggle values in the stack. The first is that such programs are difficult to write. Developing the program takes significantly longer. The second disadvantage is that you will find it very difficult to debug the program, or to modify it later. Therefore, unless you will use the program very frequently or unless there is an urgent need not to disturb the data registers, this kind of programming is not worth your time. Of course, if you are one of the many people who take pleasure in constructing the best possible program, you can consider your time an investment to improve your programming skills.

Now to develop the program. First, assume as before that the value c is in X, b is in Y, and a is in Z. This allows a natural order of data entry by the user of the program.

The calculation starts by evaluating b/2a and c/a. The value a will be used twice here, but the LASTX register provides an easy way to do this. We compute c/a, then b/2a. The steps needed are shown below, together with a "stack analysis" that illustrates the contents of the stack at each step.

Function	LASTX	X	Y	Z	T
LBL A	-	c	b	a	-
X<>Y	-	b	c	a	-
RDN	-	c	a	-	b
X<>Y	-	a	c	-	b
/	a	c/a	-	b	b
R↑	a	b	c/a	-	b
LASTX	a	a	b	c/a	-
ENTER	a	a	a	b	c/a
+	a	2a	b	c/a	c/a
/	2a	b/2a	c/a	c/a	c/a

The first few stack manipulations allow c/a to be calculated before b/a. Then the **R↑** instruction brings b back to X for the calculation of b/2a. One "trick" is used: a+a is calculated instead of 2a because it is significantly faster.

The rest of the program computes the determinant $D=(b/2a)^2-(c/a)$ and checks whether D is negative, indicating that the roots are complex numbers. If D is non-negative, the two results x_1=(-b/2a)+SQRT(D) and x_2=(-b/2a)-SQRT(D) are computed. The LASTX register is used to duplicate the value of D during this computation.

If D is negative, then the result is given in two parts. The real part, (-b/2a), is in the X register, while the magnitude of the imaginary part, SQRT(D), is given in Y. GRAD mode is set to indicate this condition; otherwise DEG mode is set.

Here is the rest of the program:

Function	LASTX	X	Y	Z	T
CHS	2a	-b/2a	c/a	c/a	c/a
ENTER	2a	-b/2a	-b/2a	c/a	c/a
RDN	2a	-b/2a	c/a	c/a	-b/2a
x^2	-b/2a	$(b/2a)^2$	c/a	c/a	-b/2a
-	-b/2a	-D	c/a	-b/2a	-b/2a
X>0	-b/2a	-D	c/a	-b/2a	-b/2a
GTO 9	-b/2a	-D	c/a	-b/2a	-b/2a
DEG	-b/2a	-D	c/a	-b/2a	-b/2a
ABS	-D	D	c/a	-b/2a	-b/2a
SQRT	D	SQRT(D)	c/a	-b/2a	-b/2a
R↑	D	-b/2a	SQRT(D)	c/a	-b/2a
X<>Y	D	SQRT(D)	-b/2a	c/a	-b/2a
-	SQRT(D)	x_2	c/a	-b/2a	-b/2a
LASTX	SQRT(D)	SQRT(D)	x_2	c/a	-b/2a
R↑	SQRT(D)	-b/2a	SQRT(D)	x_2	c/a
+	-b/2a	x_1	x_2	c/a	c/a
RTN		x_1	x_2		
LBL 9	-b/2a	|D|	c/a	-b/2a	-b/2a
SQRT	|D|	SQRT(|D|)	c/a	-b/2a	-b/2a
R↑	|D|	-b/2a	SQRT(|D|)	c/a	-b/2a
GRAD	|D|	-b/2a	SQRT(|D|)	c/a	-b/2a
RTN		-b/2a	SQRT(|D|)		

On an HP-10, you have no **R↑** instruction. You can either use three **RDN** instructions or you can rewrite the program to use a data register or two. Another difference is that you will use a line number rather than a label as the object of the **GTO** instruction.

4.3.3 The indirect operations

One of the least understood but most important capabilities of most HP programmable calculators is indirect addressing, designated by the mysterious **(i)** key on Series 10 keyboards. [On the HP-41, the shift key is used to indicate indirect addressing. Check your Owner's Manual.] When used in combination with **ISG/DSE** loop control, indirect addressing allows you to write very short programs to perform the same operations on a set of registers.

The way you use indirect addressing on HP calculators is consistent with the principle of Reverse Polish Notation that the numbers precede the operation. For example, you put in the X register a number to be stored. You put the number of the data register in a special register called the I (index) register. Then if you execute **STO(i)** the number in X will be stored into R_I, the register designated by the contents of the index register. [On the HP-15 and HP-41, other registers can be used as index registers, but the principle is the same.]

As a simple example of the power of indirect addressing, suppose you want to add the same number to registers 5 through 11. Assume that the number to be added is in X at the start of the program.

The following short sequence does the job:

```
LBL A
5.011
STO I      Initialize the index register.
RDN        The number to be added.
LBL 0      Top of loop.
STO+(i)    Add number to register contents.
ISG        On the HP-15, use ISG I.
GTO 0      Loop until greater than 11.
RTN
```

On the HP-15, you can do arithmetic while recalling registers. Try replacing the **STO+(i)** instruction with **RCL+(i)**. If you then start the program with zero in X, what is the result?

4.3.4 Testing your program

Every time you key a program into memory you must test its operation for correctness. Even if you have previously debugged the program, there is always the possibility that one of the instructions was mis-keyed.

If your trial run of the program gives an incorrect result, you could switch into program mode and attempt to check the program's numeric codes for correctness. This is quite tedious, except on the HP-41 where the program instructions are spelled out by their true names.

A better way to debug your program is to use the step by step execution capability of the calculator. While you press the **SST** (single-step) key, you can compare each result with what you expect from your program listing. If your program listing is accompanied by a numerical example showing all the intermediate results, so much the better.

When you see an intermediate result that is not correct, you can quickly find the incorrect instruction by switching into program mode. You may have to press **BST** (back-step) once or twice if you did not recognize the incorrect result immediately.

If you are developing a long program, you can insert **PSE** (pause) or **R/S** instructions to display intermediate results. These instructions can be deleted once the program is working.

Naturally, a step by step stack analysis like the one in the previous section is a very valuable tool for debugging. If your program uses a lot of memory registers you may need to record the usage of data registers as well. If you do analyze the usage of data registers, you may find that you can save program steps by frequent use of the **X<>** (exchange) instruction on the HP-15.

Finally, do not forget that except for the HP-41, these calculators can only hold one program at a time. Nevertheless, it is possible to merge two programs as long as the **GTO** and **LBL** instructions do not conflict with each other. To eliminate conflicts, you should know how the **GTO** or **GSB** instructions search for their corresponding labels. [This discussion does not apply to the HP-10 or 12, which use line numbers instead of labels.] The search proceeds downward from the **GTO** or **GSB** until the label is found. If the bottom of the program is encountered, the search continues from line 000.

You can use this label search feature to your advantage. A label can be re-used as long as its **GTO**s or **GSB**s precede it in the program and as long as the label precedes the line at which it is needed next. The structure for re-use of labels looks like this:

```
GTO 1 ... ... LBL 1 ... GTO 1 ... ... LBL 1
 |______________↑        |______________↑
```

CHAPTER 5

Application Programs

5.1 Initialize a block of data registers

This short program loads a block of data registers beginning at R_{bbb} and ending at R_{eee} with a single value. Just key in the value to be loaded, then **ENTER**, then put the register index of the form bbb.eee in the X register, and press **GSB A**.

LBL B	Clear a block of registers
0	Value to be loaded
X<>Y	
LBL A	Load a block of registers
STO I	Store bbb.eee in I
RDN	Value to be loaded is now in X
LBL 0	
STO (i)	Store value in R_I
ISG	(use **ISG I** on the HP-15)
GTO 0	Loop until R_{eee} is passed
RTN	

For example, to load the value 1 in registers 4 through 7, press

1 **ENTER** 4.007 **GSB A** .

To clear a block of registers, key in the register index and press **GSB B** . This simply loads the value 0 in all the registers in the block.

As an exercise, you may want to replace the **ISG** instruction with a **DSE** instruction. Instead of bbb.eee, you will then need to use a register index of the form eee.(bbb-1). This will save some time when initializing a block that begins with register 1. In fact, if you have an HP-16, you will need to use **DSZ** to make the program usable.

5.2 View a block of data registers

This simple routine uses **ISG** to show you the contents of each register of a block. Just put the bbb.eee index in X and press **GSB C**.

LBL C	
STO I	Store index in I
LBL 1	
RCL (i)	Recall R_I
PSE	Pause to display value
ISG	(use **ISG I** on the HP-15)
GTO 1	Continue until eee is reached
RTN	

For example, to view the contents of registers 2 and 5, press

2.005 **GSB C** .

Of course, you can substitute **DSE** or **DSZ** for **ISG**, using an index of the form eee.(bbb-1).

5.3 Pseudo-random numbers

This routine generates pseudo-random numbers that are uniformly distributed in the interval between 0 and 1. (The numbers are not truly random, because you will always get the same sequence if you start the program the same way.)

To use this routine, key in a "seed" number between 0 and 1, preferably containing 8 to 10 digits. Press **GSB E** to store the seed in register 0. Then, each time you need a new random number, press **GSB A**. Delete the previous programs before keying this one in (**LBL A** is duplicated).

LBL E	
STO 0	Store initial seed
RTN	

```
LBL A
RCL 0      Recall the current number
9821       (this step uses 4 lines)
*
.211327    (this step uses 7 lines)
+
FRAC
STO 0      Store new random number
RTN
```

For example, try a seed of .624518534, which is to be stored in register 0 (**GSB E**). Then the series of random numbers generated by **GSB A** is:

.607849
.896356
.323603
.316390

Different calculator models may give different results, depending on their internal precision. This random number generator is somewhat longer than others, but it is better behaved. It was used in the PPC ROM for the HP-41 (see Appendix B).

If program space is limited, this less sophisticated uniform random number generator may be sufficient for your needs:

```
LBL A
RCL 0      Recall the current number
->DEG      Multiply by 180/PI
FRAC       Retain fractional part
STO 0      Save the new number
RTN
```

The next program section uses the uniform random number program to generate Gaussian (normally distributed) random numbers with zero mean and variance 1.

```
LBL B
GSB A    (Execute the uniform generator)
360
*
GSB A
LN
ENTER
+
CHS
SQRT
P->R
RTN
```

This routine actually produces two Gaussian random numbers, one in X and one in Y. For example, with a seed of .624518534 again, the Gaussian random numbers are, rounded to 6 digits:

X	Y
-.364442	-.293287
-.676853	1.357730
-.440438	.062636

Again, the exact numbers you get depend on the calculator model. To get a variance v^2, multiply the result by v. To get a mean m, add m.

5.4 Fibonacci numbers

Fibonacci numbers are a series of integers in which each number is the sum of the two preceding numbers. The first two numbers of the series are 1 and 1. Thus

1+1 = 2
1+2 = 3
2+3 = 5
3+5 = 8
5+8 = 13

etc.

Here is a program to generate the series:

```
LBL A
FIX 0     Display integers
1
ENTER     Start with 1 in Y
CLX       and 0 in X
LBL 0
+         Add two numbers
PSE       Pause to display new number
LSTX      Get last number from LASTX
X<>Y      New number in X, old in Y
GTO 0     Repeat until user presses R/S
```

5.5 Permutations

The permutation function

$$P(n,k) = n!/(n-k)!$$
$$= n(n-1)(n-2)\ldots(n-k+1)$$

gives the number of different arrangements (orderings) of all subsets of k items taken from a set of n items. If you are unfamiliar with the "!" notation, see section 5.12.1 for an explanation of the factorial function. P(n,k) is available on the keyboards of the HP-11 and 15, but many other machines, including the HP-41, lack this valuable function. To compute P(n,k) on calculators lacking the factorial function, key in

n **ENTER** k **GSB A** .

Here is the program listing:

	L	X	Y	Z	T
LBL A		k	n		
1		1	k	n	
ENTER		1	1	k	n
*****		1	k	n	n
RDN		k	n	n	1
-		n-k	n	1	
X<>Y		n	n-k	1	
LBL 1		n-i	n-k	p_{i-1}	
X=Y					
GTO 2		(Quit when x reaches n-k)			
ENTER		n-i	n-i	n-k	p_{i-1}
R↑		p_{i-1}	n-i	n-i	n-k
*****		p_i	n-i	n-k	n-k
RDN		n-i	n-k	n-k	p_i
X<>Y		n-k	n-i		
RDN		n-i	n-k	p_i	
1		1	n-i	n-k	p_i
-		n-(i+1)	n-k	p_i	p_i
GTO 1					
LBL 2					
R↑		p_k			
RTN					

As an example, the number of permutations of 7 items taken from a set of 52 items is

$52 * 51 * 50 * 49 * 48 * 47 * 46 = 6.7427 \times 10^{11}$.

(The first item can be chosen 52 ways, the second 51 ways, etc.). To check this result, press

52 **ENTER** 7 **GSB A**

5.6 Combinations

The combination function

$$C(n,k) = n!/k!(n-k)!$$

$$= \frac{n(n-1)(n-2)\ldots(n-k+1)}{k(k-1)(k-2)\ldots(k-k+1)}$$

gives the number of different subsets (without regard to ordering) of k items taken from a set of n items. C(n,k), like the permutation function, is built into the HP-11 and 15. For other machines, including the HP-41, you need to use a program. To use this C(n,k) program, key in

n **ENTER** k **GSB B** .

Here is the program listing:

	I	X	Y	Z	T
LBL B		k	n		
STO I	k				
RDN		n			
1		1	n		
X<>Y		n	1		
ENTER		n	n	1	
LBL 1	k-i	n-i	n-i	C(n,i)	
RCL I		k-i	n-i	n-i	C(n,i)
/		(n-i)/(k-i)	n-i	C(n,i)	C(n,i)
R↑					
*****		C(n,i+1)	n-i		
X<>Y					
1					
-		n-(i+1)	C(n,i+1)		
ENTER		n-(i+1)	n-(i+1)	C(n,i+1)	
DSE (or **DSZ**)					
GTO 1	(Continue until k-i reaches 0)				
RDN					
RDN		C(n,k)			
RTN					

As an example, the number of combinations of 5 items taken from a set of 12 is

$$\frac{12*11*10*9*8}{5*4*3*2*1} = 792 \cdot$$

5.7 Greatest common divisor

To find the largest common factor of two numbers x and y, key in

y **ENTER** x **GSB A**

using this program:

LBL A MOD LSTX X<>Y X≠0 GTO A + RTN

This clever routine was written by John Kennedy. If you do not have a **MOD** key on your calculator, use this alternate version:

LBL A ENTER ENTER - RDN X<>Y LSTX /
LSTX RDN INT * - X≠0 GTO A + RTN

This uses the **MOD** routine from section 6.14.

The program makes use of the fact that any common factor of x and y must also be a factor of x MOD y and y MOD x. Similarly, any common factor of y MOD x and x must be a factor of x MOD (y MOD x). THe program continues in this recursive fashion, calculating (y MOD x) MOD (x MOD (y MOD x)), etc. until a remainder of zero is found. At this point, the greatest common divisor is in Y, from which the + instruction extracts it.

5.8 Sum of the digits of an integer

This short program accepts an integer in the X register and adds its digits:

LBL A STO 1 STO-1 LBL 0 10 / STO+1 INT
STO-1 X≠0 GTO 0 10 STO*1 RCL 1 RTN

For example, put 1234556789 in X, and run the program to get the result, 50. This program was written by John Kennedy.

This program uses a valuable trick. The sequence

STO 1 STO-1

is used only to clear register 1. The advantage of this over the more standard **CLX STO 1** is that it clears register 1 without disturbing the stack.

The rest of the program starts by dividing the number by 10. This leaves one digit to the right of the decimal point. The sequence **STO+1 INT STO-1** adds the fractional part of X to register 1, and replaces X by its integer part. The loop repeats this procedure, dividing by 10 and adding the fractional part (one digit) to register 1, until all the digits have been processed and the number in X is 0. Then register 1 contains 0.1 times the sum of the digits in the original number. The last 3 lines leave the sum of the digits in both register 1 and the X register.

On the HP-10, you have no instruction for **X≠0**. You can use the **X=0** instruction instead as shown below.

X=0 GTOxx GTOyy (line xx)

5.9 Convert a real number to an integer or a decimal fraction

The following sequence converts a real number to an integer by multiplying by 10 until there is no fractional part. For example, 123.45 would be converted to 12345:

LBL A INT LSTX X=Y RTN 10 * GTO A

The stopping criterion is INT(x)=x, meaning that there is no fractional part of x.

The sequence below converts a real number to a fraction by dividing by 10 until there is no integer part. For example, 123.45 would be converted to 0.12345:

LBL B FRAC LSTX X=Y RTN 10 / GTO B

This program works analogously to the previous one. The stopping rule is FRAC(x)=x.

5.10 Reverse an integer

This program, written by James Davidson, reverses the digits of an integer in the X register:

LBL A STO 1 STO-1 LBL 0 FRAC STO+1 LSTX INT 10 STO*1 / X≠0 GTO 0 RCL 1 RTN

This program starts by clearing register 1, then it enters a loop. In this loop, the number is divided by 10, the fractional part is added to register 1, and register 1 is multiplied by 10. This multiplication shifts the previous digits to the left one position and moves the last digit to the left of the decimal point. When all the digits have been processed, X is zero and the result is recalled from register 1.

5.11 Decimal to fraction conversion

These routines are handy if you have to work with fractions of inches. The problem with inches is, of course, that your calculator cannot multiply 2-11/16 inches by 3 and come up with 8-1/16. This program helps you do that by quickly converting a fraction to a decimal number which can be used in any calculation. Then another section of the program can convert the decimal number back to a fraction.

The **LBL A** section below converts a fraction to a decimal number. Load the stack with

integer part **ENTER** numerator
ENTER denominator,

then press

GSB A .

The decimal result will appear in X.

The **LBL B** section converts a decimal number to a fraction, with a maximum error of ±1/64. Just put the number in X and press

GSB B .

The fractional result appears in three parts. The integer part is in X, the numerator is in Y, and the denominator (2, 4, 8, 16, or 32) is in Z. Press **RDN** to see the numerator, and **RDN** again to see the denominator.

```
LBL A  /  +  RTN  LBL B  INT  LSTX  FRAC
32  *  LSTX  X<>Y  ENTER  FRAC  +  INT
X=Y  GTO 3  LBL 1  2  /  ENTER  FRAC  X≠0
GTO 2  RDN  X<>Y  2  /  X<>Y  GTO 1  LBL 2
/  R↑  RTN  LBL 3  CLX  R↑  1  +  RTN
```

As an example, divide 8-1/16 by 3. Press

8 **ENTER** 1 **ENTER** 16 **GSB A** .

The result is 8.0625. Next press

3 **/** .

Now convert back to a fraction:

GSB B .

The result is

2 **(RDN)** 11 **(RDN)** 16,

or 2-11/16.

5.12 Factorial calculations

Factorial calculations in the following sections illustrate some of the general techniques that can be used in solving problems on a programmable calculator.

5.12.1 The factorial function

The quickest way to obtain a very large number on an HP-10, 11, or 15 is to press

69 **x!** (use **n!** on the HP-10).

The result is $1.711224524 \times 10^{98}$. Perhaps the notation **!** refers to the surprisingly rapid increase of the factorial function.

The factorial function of an integer n is the result of the multiplication of all the integers from 1 to n:

$$n! = 1 * 2 * \ldots * n .$$

This function can be generalized for non-integers. It is called the gamma function, with GAMMA(n+1)=n! if n is an integer. Consult a good advanced mathematics text if you are interested in the properties of the gamma function.

5.12.2 n! for any n

If you need to know **n!** for a number greater than 69, this routine will calculate it. Instead of multiplying all the numbers from 1 to n, this program adds the logarithms of all the numbers from 1 to n, using the mathematical identity:

log(n!)=log(1*2*...*n)=log(1)+log(2)+...+log(n).

The fractional part of log(n!) is converted back to a mantissa, so that the result is

$$n! = x \; 10^y,$$

where x and y are the numbers left in the X and Y registers at the completion of the program. The result in x is called the mantissa, and y is called the characteristic. To use the program, just key in an integer and press **R/S**:

	I	L	X	Y	Z	T
LBL A			n			
X=0						
1		Calculate 1! for 0!				
STO I	n					
0			0			
LBL 1	i	S_{i+1}=log(n)+...+log(i+1))				
RCL I			i	S_{i+1}		
LOG			log(i)			
+			S_i			
DSE (or **DSZ**)		Continue until i reaches zero				
GTO 1	i-1					
		S_n=log(n)+...+log(1)=log(n!)				
INT		log(n)!	y			
LSTX			log(n!)	y		
FRAC						
10^x			x	y		
RTN						

On the HP-15, use **DSE I** instead of **DSE**. The program is quite slow, but its results are reasonably accurate. For example, if x=5, the result $5!=1.200000003\text{x}10^2$ appears after about 5 seconds. The actual result is 120.

The first few steps in the program take care of the special case 0!=1 by replacing a 0 with 1. The number n is then stored in the index register, so that it can be used to control the DSE loop. Each time through the loop, log(i) is added to the subtotal, for i=n, n-1,...,1.

The structure of this program is quite straightforward. It is another example of the power and simplicity that the **DSE** instruction provides.

5.12.3 Inverse factorial function

Suppose you have a number x 10^y, and you want to find the smallest number n such that n! is at least as big as x 10^y. The following program does the calculation (after you put y in the Y register and x in the X register):

LBL A LOG + 0 ENTER RDN LBL 2 R↑ 1
+ LOG LSTX RDN + X<Y GTO 2 R↑ RTN

There is a slight chance that the answer will be incorrect by one unit due to roundoff error. To be sure you have the right answer, you can use a non-integer value for x. For example, use 119.99 instead of 120.

The program works much the same as the previous one, computing log(i!) for increasing values of i, until log(x) is equalled or exceeded. Log(x) is held in the Y register, and the sum log(1)+log(2)+...+log(i) is held in the X register. The number i is held in stack register T, accessible by R↑. Each time through the loop, log(i+1) is added to the sum, and i is replaced by i+1 and rolled-down into the T register. The new sum is compared to log(x), and the loop is repeated until log(x) is equalled or exceeded. Then a R↑ instruction brings the result i back into the X register.

5.12.4 Stirling's approximation

Stirling's formula is an approximation to n! (and to the gamma function of n+1) that becomes increasingly good as n becomes larger. For n=69, the accuracy is 4 to 5 digits. The formula is:

$n! = (2\ PI)^{1/2}\ n^{n+1/2}\ e^{-n+1/12n}$, or equivalently,

$\ln(n!) = (1/2)\ln(2\ PI) + (n+1/2)\ln(n) - n + 1/12n$,

and $\log(n!) = \ln(n!)/\ln(10)$.

Despite the complexity of the formula, the program is quite simple and fast, because no looping is needed:

	L	X	Y	Z	T
LBL C		n			
ENTER					
ENTER					
LN		ln(n)	n	n	
.5		.5	ln(n)	n	n
R↑		n	.5	ln(n)	n
+		(n+.5)	ln(n)	n	n
*****		(n+.5)ln(n)	n	n	n
X<>Y					
-		(n+.5)ln(n)-n			

```
LSTX        n
12
*           12n
1/x         1/12n
+           (n+.5)ln(n)-n+1/12n
PI          PI
ENTER       PI    PI
+           2PI
LN          ln(2PI)
2
/           .5ln(2PI)
+           .5ln(2PI)+(n+.5)ln(n)-n+1/12n
10
LN
/           ln(n!)/ln(10) = log(n!)
INT         log(n!)  y
LSTX        log(n!)  y
FRAC
10^x        x    y
RTN
```

You just put the number n in the X register and execute the program. The result is in two parts, x in the X register and y in the Y register, with

$n! \cong x\ 10^y$.

The mantissa is in X, and the exponent in Y. For example, for 8! the result is

$8! \cong 4.032021804 \times 10^4$,

compared to the true value of 4032. A major advantage of this program is that the execution time is roughly the same for all values of n.

The program first calculates ln(n), then (n+1/2)ln(n). Next n is subtracted, 1/12n is added, and (1/2)ln(2 PI) is added. Dividing by ln(10) gives log(n!). The fractional part of this logarithm is converted into the mantissa, while the integer part is the characteristic.

If you have an HP-10, which has no **R↑** function, you can start the program with **STO 0** rather than **ENTER ENTER** to store the value of n. Then replace the R↑ instruction with **RCL 0.**

5.13 Root-finding

One frequent application of programmable calculators is solving equations of the form f(x)=0; that is, finding the value of x that makes this equation true for a user-supplied function f. For example, suppose that you need to find the value of x for which 2x=ln((x+1)/(x-1)). Just rearrange the equation to be 2x-ln((x+1)/(x-1))=0, which is of the form f(x)=0.

Minimization and maximization problems can also be solved in the form f(x)=0 by using the appropriate first derivative function for f.

A root-finder is built into the HP-15 and 34 calculators, but for other machines you will need a program. The root finder program given here uses Newton's method, which generally produces fast convergence. It can fail in some cases, but you will not normally encounter such situations.

Given the previous two root estimates x_n and x_{n-1}, the formula for the next root estimate is $x_{n+1} = x_n - (x_n - x_{n-1}) f(x_n)/(f(x_n) - f(x_{n-1}))$. This formula is applied repeatedly until x_{n+1} is the same as x_n, **within the current display rounding accuracy.**

Here is the root finder program, together with a stack and data register analysis:

	X	Y	Z	R0	R1	R2
LBL A						
STO 0	x_1	x_1-x_0		x_1		
EEX						
2						
/	$.01x_1$					
X<>Y	x_1-x_0	$.01x_1$				
X=0						
X<>Y						
STO 1					x_1-x_0	
CLX	0					
STO 2						0
LBL 9				x_n	x_n-x_{n-1}	f_{n-1}
RCL 0	x_n					
PSE	(optional)					
GSB B	f_n					
ST-2						$f_{n-1}-f_n$
STO*1					$(x_n-x_{n-1})f_n$	
RCL 1	$(x_n-x_{n-1})f_n$	f_n				
RCL 2	$f_{n-1}-f_n$	$(x_n-x_{n-1})f_n$	f_n			
X≠0						
/	$(x_n-x_{n-1})f_n/(f_{n-1}-f_n)$	f_n				
STO 1					$x_{n+1}-x_n$	
RDN	f_n					
STO 2						f_n
RCL 0	x_n					
RND	$\mathrm{RND}(x_n)$					
LSTX	x_n					
RCL 1	$x_{n+1}-x_n$	x_n				
+	x_{n+1}	$\mathrm{RND}(x_n)$				
STO 0				x_{n+1}		
RND	$\mathrm{RND}(x_{n+1})$	$\mathrm{RND}(x_n)$				
X≠Y						

GTO 9		x_{n+1}	$x_{n+1}-x_n$	f_n-f_{n+1}
LSTX	x_{n+1}			
RTN				

To use this root-finding program, you need to write an instruction sequence starting with **LBL B** that accepts a number in the X register and returns the value f(x) in the X register. This sequence should not alter the values in registers 0, 1, or 2, and it should not contain a **LBL 9** instruction. (Of course, you could rewrite the root-finder to use different numbered registers if there is a conflict.) For the example $f(x)=2x-\ln((x+1)/(x-1))$ you can use the sequence:

	LASTX	X	Y	Z	T
LBL B		x			
ENTER		x	x		
ENTER		x	x	x	
ENTER		x	x	x	x
1		1	x	x	x
+	1	x+1	x	x	x
X<>Y		x	x+1	x	x
LSTX		1	x	x+1	x
-		x-1	x+1	x	x
/		(x+1)/(x-1)	x	x	
LN		ln((x+1)/(x-1))	x	x	
-		x-ln((x+1)/(x-1))	x		
+		2x-ln((x+1)/(x-1))			
RTN					

This program makes use of the automatic duplication of stack register T when the stack drops. The first several steps of the program push the value of n up to the top of the stack.

Once you have the f(x) sequence prepared and

tested, you are ready to start the root finder.

Key in an initial step size, **ENTER**, an initial guess for the root x, then press **GSB A** to start the root-finder. The initial step size is optional. If you enter 0 as the step size, the program will use 1% of the initial guess as the initial step size. For the example given above, try

0 **ENTER** 1.1 **GSB A** .

You will see the series of estimates:

1.100000
1.089000
1.169700
1.191627
1.199193
1.199671
1.199679
1.199679

Note that convergence becomes more rapid as the program gets closer to the true root.

5.14 Financial calculations

One of the most commonly encountered financial problems is to calculate missing components of a level-payment cash flow, such as a mortgage. Although this capability is built into the HP-12, this problem requires a program on most other HP calculators. The program presented here is intended to simulate the basic features of a level-payment financial calculator.*

A level-payment cash flow has five variables: the number of payments **N**, interest rate **I** (percent per period), present value **PV**, payment per period **PMT**, and future value **FV**. The last three of these variables can be either positive or negative. Positive numbers indicate cash received; negative numbers indicate cash paid out. If you know four of the five variables the program presented here will calculate the missing component needed to balance the present values of the inflow and outflow.

To use the program, first store the four known components in the corresponding registers:

register	1	2	3	4	5
value	N	I	PV	PMT	FV

Then press **GSB y**, where **y** is the register number (1 to 5) of the unknown parameter.

For example, consider a mortgage of $100,000 at 11% per year for 30 years (360 months). Since the payments are made monthly, you need to convert the interest rate to a monthly rate of 11/12%. Here is the full solution:

360 **STO 1** (360 payments)
11 **ENTER** 12 / **STO 2** (11/12% per month)
100000 **STO 3** ($100,000 received at start)
0 **STO 5** (no money paid at end of loan)
GSB 4 (solve for PMT)

The result is a monthly payment of -$952.32, negative because money is being paid out.

The formulas used in the program are all derived from the basic equation:

$$FV + PV(1+i)^N + PMT[(1+i)^N-1]/i = 0$$

(Here $i = I/100$ is a fraction.) This equation can be solved for each of the individual parameters except i:

$$N = \ln[(PMT/i-FV)/(PMT/i+PV)]/\ln(1+i)$$
$$PV = -FV(1+i)^{-N} - (PMT/i)[1-(1+i)^{-N}]$$
$$PMT = -i[PV + (FV+PV)/((1+i)^N-1)]$$
$$FV = -PV - (PV+PMT/i)[(1+i)^N-1]$$

To solve for i, the basic equation can be viewed as

a problem of the form $f(i)=0$ and solved by Newton's tangent method. Starting with an estimate i_n of i, the next estimate i_{n+1} can be computed as

$$i_{n+1} = i_n + f(i_n)/f'(i_n), \text{ where}$$
$$f(i_n) = FV + PV + (PV+PMT/i)[(1+i)^{N-1}], \text{ and}$$
$$f'(i_n) = N(1+i)^{N-1}(PV+PMT/i) - (PMT/i^2)[(1+i)^{N-1}]$$

The initial guess is

$$i_0 = |PMT|/(|PV|+|FV|) + (|PV|+|FV|)/(N^3|PMT|),$$

a formula developed by Don Dewey for the financial calculation program in the PPC ROM (see Appendix B).

Here is the program, with a stack analysis:

	LASTX	X	Y	Z	T
LBL 0					
CLX	(This segment merely initializes				
STO 1	the five registers to zero)				
STO 2					
STO 3					
STO 4					
STO 5					
RTN					
LBL 1					
GSB 7	i	PMT/i	1+i	$(1+i)^N$	$(1+i)^N$
ENTER		PMT/i	PMT/i	1+i	
X<>Y	(enables stack lift)				
RCL 5		FV	PMT/i	PMT/i	1+i
-		PMT/i-FV	PMT/i	1+i	
X<>Y		PMT/i	PMT/i-FV		
RCL 3		PV	PMT/i	PMT/i-FV	1+i
+		PMT/i+PV	PMT/i-FV	1+i	
/					
LN		ln[(PMT/i+PV)/(PMT/i-FV)]			
X<>Y					
LN		ln(1+i)			
/					

	LASTX	X	Y	Z	T
STO 1		$\ln[(PMT/i+PV)/(PMT/i-FV)]/\ln(1+i)$			
RTN					
LBL 2					
RCL 4					
ABS		$\lvert PMT\rvert$			
RCL 3					
ABS		$\lvert PV\rvert$	$\lvert PMT\rvert$		
RCL 5					
ABS		$\lvert FV\rvert$	$\lvert PV\rvert$	$\lvert PMT\rvert$	
+					
/		$\lvert PMT\rvert/(\lvert FV\rvert+\lvert PV\rvert)$			
ENTER					
1/x		$(\lvert FV\rvert+\lvert PV\rvert)/\lvert PMT\rvert$	$\lvert PMT\rvert/(\lvert FV\rvert+\lvert PV\rvert)$		
RCL 1					
ENTER		N	N		
x^2		N^2			
*****		N^3			
/					
+		i_0			
EEX					
2					
x					
STO 2		I_0			
LBL 6					
RCL 3					
STO 0	(Register 0 will be used to form PV+PMT/i)				
GSB 7	i	PMT/i	1+i	$(1+i)^N$	$(1+i)^N$
STO+0					
LSTX					
/		PMT/i^2			
RDN					
/		$(1+i)^{N-1}$	$(1+i)^N$	PMT/i^2	
X<>Y					
1					

	LASTX	X	Y	Z	T
-					
ENTER		$(1+i)^N-1$	$(1+i)^N-1$	$(1+i)^{N-1}$	PMT/i^2
R↑					
*		$PMT/i^2[(1+i)^N-1]$	$(1+i)^N-1$	$(1+i)^{N-1}$	
R↑					
RCL 1					
*		$(1+i)^{N-1}(PV+PMT/i)$	$PMT/i^2[(1+i)^N-1]$	$(1+i)^N-1$	
RCL 0					
*		$N(1+i)^{N-1}(PV+PMT/i)$			
-		$f'(i)$	$(1+i)^N-1$		
X<>Y					
RCL 0					
*		$(PV+PMT/i)(1+i)^N-1$	$f'(i)$		
RCL 3					
+					
RCL 5					
+		$f(i)$	$f'(i)$		
X<>Y					
/		$f(i)/f'(i)$			
EEX					
2					
*		$I_{n+1}-I_n$			
RCL 2		I_n			
RND					
X<>Y		$I_{n+1}-I_n$	$RND(I_n)$		
LSTX		I_n			
+		I_{n+1}			
STO 2					
RND		$RND(I_{n+1})$	$RND(I_n)$		
X≠Y?					
GTO 6					
LSTX		I_{n+1}			
RTN					
LBL 3					

	LASTX	X	Y	Z	T
GSB 7	i	PMT/i	1+i	$(1+i)^N$	$(1+i)^N$
RCL 5					
R↑		$(1+i)^N$	FV	PMT/i	1+i
/					
X<>Y		PMT/i	$FV(1+i)^{-N}$		
1					
LSTX		$(1+i)^N$	1	PMT/i	$FV(1+i)^{-N}$
1/x					
-		$1-(1+i)^{-N}$	PMT/i	$FV(1+i)^{-N}$	
*					
+					
CHS					
STO 3		$-[FV(1+i)^{-N}+(PMT/i)(1-(1+i)^{-N})]$			
RTN					
LBL 4					
GSB 7	i	PMT/i	1+i	$(1+i)^N$	$(1+i)^N$
LSTX					
R↑		$(1+i)^N$	i		
RCL 5					
RCL 3					
+		FV+PV	$(1+i)^N$	i	
X<>Y					
1					
-		$(1+i)^N-1$	FV+PV	i	
/					
RCL 3					
+		$PV+(FV+PV)/[(1+i)^N-1]$	i		
*					
CHS					
STO 4		$-i(PV+(FV+PV)/[(1+i)^N-1])$			
RTN					
LBL 5					
GSB 7	i	PMT/i	1+i	$(1+i)^N$	$(1+i)^N$
RCL 3					

	LASTX	X	Y	Z	T
+					
R↑		$(1+i)^N$	PV+PMT/i		
1					
-					
*		$(PV+PMT/I)[(1+i)^N-1]$			
RCL 3					
+					
CHS					
STO 5		$-PV-(PV+PMT/I)[(1+i)^N-1]$			
RTN					
LBL 7					
1		1			
RCL 2		I	1		
%		i	1		
+		1+i			
RCL 1		N			
y^x		$(1+i)^N$			
RCL 4		PMT			
1					
RCL 2		I	1	PMT	$(1+i)^N$
%		i	1		
+	i	1+i	PMT	$(1+i)^N$	
X<>Y					
LSTX		i	PMT	1+i	$(1+i)^N$
/	i	PMT/i	1+i	$(1+i)^N$	$(1+i)^N$
RTN					

As another example, let's calculate the annual percentage rate on the $100,000 mortgage if you have to pay an loan origination fee ("points") of $2000:

2000 **STO-3** (only $98000 is actually received)

GSB 2 (solve for the real interest rate)

The result is an interest rate of 0.93805% per

month, or 11.26% per year.

One more example. Suppose you want to repay the loan after 5 years. What is the balance?

60 **STO 1** (5 years = 60 months)

GSB 5 (calculate the remaining balance due)

The result is -$95,356.60, indicating that you have to pay this amount of money to cancel the loan.

5.15 Time for a game

This next program will allow you to journey through time! Alas, your time machine is not fully perfected. You can only specify the maximum possible jump. The direction and size of the jump is random, up to the specified maximum.

Your goal is to reach a precise year in the fewest possible jumps. Key in a "seed" value between 0 and 1 for the random number generator, **ENTER**, the starting year, **ENTER**, the target year, then **R/S**.

The calculator will halt with the starting year in the display. Key in the maximum jump and press **R/S** again. The display shows the year in which you have arrived. Be patient; it is indeed possible to succeed! When you do arrive, the number of jumps will be shown in FIX 2 format.

An optimum strategy exists, based on minimizing the expected logarithm of the distance to the target year. I will not spoil your fun by revealing it, though.

The program uses 4 memory registers. This helps to protect it from alteration of the stack when the program is halted for input.

```
LBL A  FIX 0  STO 2  RDN  STO 1  RDN  STO 4
 CLX  STO 3  LBL 0  1  STO+3  RCL 1  R/S
 RCL 4  9821  *  .211327  +  FRAC  STO 4
 ENTER  +  1  -  *  INT  STO+1  RCL 2
 RCL 1  X≠Y  GTO 0  RCL 3  FIX 2  RTN
```

On the HP-11 and 15, you can use the **RAN** (random number) function to replace the instructions from RCL 4 through STO 4, inclusive. You can also delete the **RDN STO 4** in the beginning part of the program. The random number generator used here was described in section 5.3.

The first part of the program, from **LBL A** to **LBL 0**, initializes the data registers. Register 1 contains the current date, register 2 the destination date, register 3 the number of jumps, and register 4 the random number (between 0 and 1).

The main part of the program is the **LBL 0/GTO 0** loop. In this loop the calculator multiplies the maximum jump size by a random number between -1 and +1, to get the actual jump size and direction. This jump is added to the current year to get the new current year. If this is not the destination year, the program returns to **LBL 0**, where 1 is added to the number of jumps and the new current year is displayed.

When the destination year is reached, the display mode is changed to FIX 2 and the number of jumps is recalled to the X register. Congratulations!

CHAPTER 6

Tips and tricks for the Series 10 machines

6.1 Exponents

It is not necessary to key in both digits of the exponent if the left one is zero. For example, 4×10^8, which displays as

4   08

can be keyed in by pressing 4 **EEX** 8.

Another tip: When you have a number with an exponent in the display, only 8 digits of the number are visible. The Series 10 machines provide a convenient way to view all 10 digits of the internal representation without actually changing the number in X. Just press and hold

f PREFIX

All 10 digits of the number will be displayed as long as you hold down the **PREFIX** key. When you release the key, the standard numeric display will return. Some earlier HP calculators have a **MANT** (mantissa) key that works the same way.

6.2 Leading zeros

When you key in a fractional number like 0.32, you do not need to key in the leading zero. Just press: .(decimal) 3 2

6.3 Avoid CLX in programs

If you use **CLX** in a program, do not depend on the stack lift being disabled. For example, when **CLX** is followed by a **RCL** instruction or a digit entry, the zero in the X register is normally overwritten with the new value. However, on some HP calculators (including the HP-41), this is not always the case. If you interrupt the program just after the **CLX** instruction, then restart it, the stack is lifted by the **RCL** and X is not overwritten. This inconsistency has been fixed on later HP machines, but it's better to be safe. Instead of using the sequence

CLX RCL n

in a program, use

RDN RCL n

This ensures that interruption and restarting of the program will not affect the result, even if you use **X<>Y** twice or **RDN** four times to review the stack.

6.4 Checking the number of registers allocated

HP's newer calculators, including the Series 10 machines, automatically reduce the number of data registers as the size of the program increases. If you have recently added to a program, you may not have enough data registers left to run the program. When you run the program, it will calculate until it hits an instruction that calls for a data register beyond the current allocation, then you will get an error message. A better approach is to put a

RCL n

instruction at the top of the program to check the needed number of data registers immediately.

If you are using the complex stack or matrix features of the HP-15, you will need to use **g MEM** to check the memory allocations for data registers, complex stack, matrix data, and programs.

6.5 Doubling a number

Use

ENTER +

instead of

2 *

It's faster.

6.6 Duplicating Y to the top of the stack

This short sequence duplicates the number in Y into the Z and T registers, without changing the number in X:

ENTER ENTER - +

If your calculator has a R↑ key, you can use the sequence

X<>Y ENTER ENTER R↑ ,

which is faster in a program, but harder to perform from the keyboard.

6.7 Rounding

To round a number to the nearest integer, the standard technique is to add 0.5 and take the integer part. However, the sequence

ENTER

FRAC

+

INT

is slightly faster. If you want to round to the nearest multiple of q (where q is something other than 1), use the sequence

q

/

LSTX

X<>Y

ENTER

FRAC

+

INT

*****

On the HP-11 and 15, there is a **RND** function that provides rounding to the current display setting. There is a potential problem with the standard form of rounding. For example, in **FIX 0** mode, all numbers that end in .5 are rounded up to the next integer. If you have a large amount of data, this could bias the average upward. Astronomers use a slightly different form of rounding, in which numbers that end in .5 are rounded up or down to an <u>even</u> number. To implement this type of rounding on the HP-11 or 15 (or 41), use the sequence

2

/

RND

ENTER

+ .

6.8 Mile/kilometer conversion

To quickly convert miles to kilometers, or vice versa, you can make use of the fact that ln(5), which is 1.6094... is within 0.01% of the true conversion factor. This was documented by Neil Murphy in V1N2 of "65 Notes".

For example, to convert 40 km to miles, press

40

ENTER

5

LN

/

6.9 Multiples of PI

To get a multiple of PI, it is often faster to use the degrees-to-radians conversion function. For example, if you need (4 PI/3), you can press

240

->RAD .

This technique was documented by Bill Kolb in "Better Programming on the HP-67/97", a publication of PPC.

As another example, to get PI/180, press

1

->RAD .

6.10 Tricks with trigonometric functions

To keep an angle within the range $-90 \leq x \leq 90$, use the sequence

SIN **SIN^{-1}** .

To keep an angle within the range $0 \leq x \leq 180$, use

COS **COS^{-1}** .

Source: Dave Wilder in "Better Programming on the HP-67/97".

If you need both the sine and the cosine of an angle, use the sequence

angle **ENTER** 1 **P-R** .

The cosine is left in X, the sine in Y.

To calculate the supplement of an angle, 180-x for x between 0 and 180 degrees, press

COS **CHS** **COS^{-1}**

Trigonometric functions provide a shortcut to compute certain special functions, provided that x is in the range $-1<x<1$.

$(1-x^2)^{1/2}$	**$\cos^{-1}$**	**SIN**
$x/(1-x^2)^{1/2}$	**$\sin^{-1}$**	**TAN**
$(1-x^2)^{1/2}/x$	**$\cos^{-1}$**	**TAN**
$1/(1-x^2)^{1/2}$	**$\tan^{-1}$**	**COS**
$x/(1+x^2)^{1/2}$	**$\tan^{-1}$**	**SIN**

Source: Bill Kolb in "Better Programming on the HP-67/97".

6.11 Hyperbolic trig functions

The HP-15 is HP's only calculator that has built-in hyperbolic trig functions. The program sequences in this section will enable you to use hyperbolics on any HP calculator.

Many of the shortcut formulas given here rely on interesting properties of the gudermannian function:

$$gd(x) = 2 \tan^{-1} e^x - PI/2$$

and the inverse gudermannian function:

$$gd^{-1}(x) = \ln \tan (PI/4 + x/2) \quad .$$

For calculations involving the gudermannian function and the inverse gudermannian function, degree mode will be assumed. This means that 90 degrees is used instead of PI/2, and 45 degrees instead of PI/4.

Hyperbolic cosine, $\cosh(x)=(e^x+e^{-x})/2$

e^x ENTER 1/x + 2 /

Hyperbolic sine, $\sinh(x)=(e^x-e^{-x})/2$

e^x ENTER 1/x - 2 /

Hyperbolic tangent, $\tanh(x)=\sin gd(x)$

e^x TAN^{-1} ENTER + 90 - SIN

Inverse hyperbolic sine, $\sinh^{-1}(x) = gd^{-1} \tan^{-1}(x)$

TAN^{-1} 2 / 45 + TAN LN

Inverse hyperbolic cosine, $\cosh^{-1}(x) = gd^{-1} \sin^{-1}(x)$

SIN^{-1} 2 / 45 + TAN LN

Inverse hyperbolic tangent, $\tanh^{-1}(x) = gd^{-1} \cos^{-1}(x)$

COS^{-1} 2 / 45 + TAN LN

6.12 Law of Cosines

Your calculator's built-in rectangular/polar coordinate conversion functions are handy for many complicated trigonometric calculations. For example, to evaluate the formula

$$c = (a^2 + b^2 - 2ab \cos C)^{1/2} ,$$

first note that this can be rewritten as

$$c = ((a \cos C - b)^2 + (a \sin C)^2)^{1/2} .$$

This leads to the simplified sequence

C **ENTER** a **P->R** b **-** **R->P** ,

to calculate the value of c. Source: Bill Kolb.

6.13 Spherical coordinates

To convert from rectangular to spherical coordinates, use the sequence

z **ENTER** y **ENTER** x

R->P ENTER CLX + R↑ R->P .

The radius r ends up in X, the z-axis angle theta in Y, and the x-y angle phi in Z. If the rectangular coordinate data is coming from data registers, you may wish to use the slightly shorter sequence

RCL y **RCL** x **R->P RCL** z **R->P** ,

which gives the same results.

To convert from spherical to rectangular coordinates, use the sequence phi **ENTER** theta **ENTER** r

P->R ENTER R↑ R↑ P->R .

The rectangular coordinate z ends up in Z, y in Y, and x in X. If you have the spherical coordinates in data registers, you can use the sequence

RCL theta **RCL** r **P->R**

X<>Y RCL phi **X<>Y P->R** .

If your calculator does not have a **R↑** function, you can use three **RDN**'s for one **R↑**, or two **RDN**'s for two **R↑**'s.

6.14 Functions not available on the keyboard

SIGN

The SIGN function replaces the number x in the X-register by -1 if x is negative, 1 if x is positive. If x is zero, the result is normally 0. However, the **SIGN** function on the HP-41 sets SIGN(0)=1, which is not consistent with the standard mathematical definition of the SIGN function.

If you can be sure that x is not zero, the SIGN function can be calculated using three steps:

ABS LSTX / .

If x may be zero, the following sequence does the job:

ABS LSTX X≠0 / , for the HP-11 or 15,

or **ABS X=0 GTO nn LSTX /** , followed by line nn for the HP-10 or 12.

MOD

The MOD (modulo) function is defined as:

a **MOD** b = a - b*INT(a/b).

The modulo function gives the remainder of the division of a by b. For example, when you divide 25 by 4, the result is 6 with a remainder of 1.

Therefore 25 **MOD** 4 is 1.

The MOD function is often useful, but it is not provided on any of the Series 10 machines. On the HP-16, no **INT** function is provided, so you cannot program a MOD function. However, the **RMD** (remainder) function is available in integer mode. To compute the MOD function, load the stack with:

a **ENTER** b ,

then press

ENTER ENTER - RDN X<>Y LSTX / INT * -

Now let's see how this sequence works. Here is the full stack analysis:

	LASTX	X	Y	Z	T
		b	a		
ENTER		b	b	a	
ENTER		b	b	b	a
-	b	0	b	a	a
RDN	b	b	a	a	0
X<>Y	b	a	b	a	0
LSTX	b	b	a	b	a
/	b	a/b	b	a	a
INT	a/b	INT(a/b)	b	a	a
*	INT(a/b)	bINT(a/b)	a	a	a
-	bINT(a/b)	a MOD b	a	a	a

Note that most of this short sequence is needed just to get the stack arranged so that X=b, Y=a, Z=b, and T=a. The rest is simple.

6.15 Combined test instructions

The HP-11 and 16 calculators (as well as the HP-41) lack tests for **X≥0** and for **X≥Y**. These are easy to simulate.

For X≥0 use: **X≠0** **X>0**

For X≥Y use: **X≠Y** **X>Y**

To see how these sequences work, consider the three possible cases:

X is negative		X is zero		X is positive	
X≠0	true	**X≠0**	false	**X≠0**	true
X>0	false	**X>0**	skipped	**X>0**	true
...	skipped	...	not skipped	...	not skipped

The line following **X>0** is skipped unless X is greater than or equal to zero. Sequential tests like this are frequently used by advanced programmers.

The technique used to create the **X≥0** and **X≥Y** tests can be generalized. To create a special test that is true if either test A or test B is true, use the sequence

inverse of test A
test B
... skipped unless A or B is true

For example, if test A is **X=0** and test B is **X>0**, the sequence **X≠0 X>0** simulates **X≥Y**.

To create a special test that is true only if both test A and test B are true, use the sequence

test A
inverse of test B
any test instruction that will be false
if test A is false or test B is false
... skipped unless both A and B are true

For example, if test A is **X≥0** (actually **X≠0 X>0**) and test B is **X≥Y**, the sequence

CF 0 X≠0 X>0 X<Y F? 0

will skip the next instruction unless $X \geq 0$ and $X \geq Y$. With 4 test instructions in a row, this is a rather unusual example, but it shows how far the concepts of combined testing can be carried.

6.16 Editing a program

If you have to modify a program that you have already written down on paper, begin from the end and work your way upward. When you work this way, adding and deleting lines only changes the line numbers in the part of the program that has already been corrected. As you work backward, you can use **BST** (backstep) to move a few steps backwards, and **GTO** to skip over more steps. When you use **GTO** to move around while editing the program, make sure you do not accidentally enter a **GTO** instruction into the program. On the HP-15, you must press **GTO CHS** followed by the 3-digit line number. On the other Series 10 machines, press **GTO**, the decimal point, then the 3-digit line number.

On the HP-10 and 12, instructions cannot be inserted and deleted. You can only over-write the existing program. On these and other "line-addressed" calculators (those that do not use labels), you might as well re-key the program starting at the first needed insertion or deletion.

One way to avoid this problem is to sprinkle **PSE** (pause) instructions throughout a program as you are developing it. The **PSE** instructions act as space fillers that can be deleted when you need to insert instructions in the program. When you have a final working version, you can re-key the program without the **PSE** steps.

6.17 Repeated execution of a program

The **RTN** instruction has the normal function in a program of marking the end of a subroutine. When the **RTN** instruction is encountered, execution continues with the line following the **GSB** instruction that called the subroutine.

If the **RTN** instruction is encountered when no subroutine was called, the program pointer is set to line 000 and execution halts. This is a convenience feature because you can then run the program again by just pressing **R/S** from the keyboard.

Keep this feature in mind when you need to put stopping instructions in your programs. If you want execution to restart at the same point, use an **R/S** instruction to stop. If you want to allow restarting from the beginning of the program, use **RTN**. You do not need to put a **RTN** at the last line of the program, because the calculator automatically does a **RTN** after the last instruction in program memory.

6.18 Solve and Integrate subroutines (HP-15)

Do not use **R/S** in a function program for Solve or Integrate. This will lead to incorrect results.

6.19 Displaying two integer numbers at once

Suppose you have two integers in the X and Y registers, and each is less than 100,000. You can display both numbers by doing:

EEX 5 / + .

This displays the former Y register contents as the

integer part, and the integer that was in X as the fractional part.

6.20 Exchanging two data registers

Suppose you want to interchange the contents of data registers 1 and 2. On the HP-15 (or on the HP-41) you can do:

X<> 1 X<> 2 X<> 1 .

This sequence preserves the stack contents. For other machines, do:

RCL 1 RCL 2 STO 1 X<>Y STO 2 .

Follow this with two **RDN** instructions if you want to bring back the original values to X and Y. The former contents of the Z and T registers are lost.

6.21 Matrix manipulation

On the HP-15, you can reduce the dimension of a matrix without losing the coefficients that you want to keep. You just need to keep in mind the order in which data registers are allocated. For example, the 9 elements of a 3x3 matrix are stored in the order: (row 1, column 1), (row 1, column 2), (row 1, column 3),..., (row 3, column 3). If you reduce the dimension to 2x3 or 3x2, only 6 elements are needed. The last three elements are lost in the redimensioning. This is correct if you are redimensioning to 2x3, but not 3x2.

The way to redimension without losing data is to transpose the matrix and/or interchange rows until the data you want to keep is in the lowest numbered rows.

For example, suppose you want to reduce a 3x3 matrix to 2x2, retaining the first two rows and columns. This requires two steps if you don't want to lose data. First reduce the dimension to 2x3, eliminating the last row. Next, transpose the matrix so that it is 3x2, with the two unwanted entries in the last row. Now you can reduce the dimension safely to 2x2. Transpose again to get the desired matrix.

Reducing the matrix dimension and resizing back to the original dimension is a quick way to zero the last row or rows. If you transpose first, you can zero the last columns.

6.22 Beware of USER mode (HP-11 and 15)

If you get an error message while trying to key **1/x**, check the display for the USER annunciator. In USER mode (when the annunciator is visible) the white functions on the key are obtained by first pressing the gold (f) shift key. You can activate or deactivate USER mode by executing the **USER** function.

6.23 Shortcuts with %

The **%** function replaces the number in X with xy/100, which is x% of y. The stack is **not** dropped as it is for almost all other two-number functions. The Y register remains undisturbed for further calculations. This allows percentages to be easily added to or subtracted from the base value.

Calculations like

n ENTER .03 *

can sometimes be replaced by

n ENTER 3 **%** .

The result is the same, but the **%** version leaves

the number n in the Y register. If you are in the middle of a calculation, this difference may force you to use the normal multiplication method.

Calculating discounts or markups is much easier with the % function. For example, to calculate $135 less 5% discount, use

135 **ENTER** 5 **%** **-** .

To calculate $49 plus 7% tax, use

49 **ENTER** 7 **%** **+** .

Another handy use of the % function is for repeated multiplication or division by 10. To multiply a number repeatedly by 10, key in the number, then press

EEX 3 **X<>Y** **%** **%** **%** **%** ...

The number 1000 remains in Y, so that each press of % produces 1000% of x, or 10 times x. To repeatedly divide a number by 10, press

EEX 1 **X<>Y** **%** **%** **%** **%** ...

This takes 10% of x each time you press **%**. This technique was first suggested by Curt Rostenback.

6.24 Polynomial Evaluation

Horner's method is a fast way to compute the value of a polynomial function. This method is best illustrated by an example. Suppose you have to evaluate the polynomial formula

$$24x^4 + 5x^3 + 7x + 9$$

for several values of x. The first step is to factor the formula:

$$(((24x+5)x)x + 7)x + 9 \quad .$$

The sequence of steps you need to evaluate this formula is

```
x
ENTER  ENTER  ENTER
24  *
5  +
*
*
7  +
*
9  +
```

The first three steps load the stack with copies of x, so that multiplication by x requires just a press of the * key. Study the alternate multiplication and addition in this example, and compare it to the factored formula. The correspondence is simple and direct.

6.25 Easy histograms

A histogram is a summary of the frequency of occurrence of different values of a random variable or any other event or function under study. The usual procedure is to divide the set of outcomes into "bins", or intervals, and to total the number of times the outcome falls within each bin.

Your calculator's indirect addressing capability makes this easy. Once you have computed the bin number, just use this sequence:

```
STO I        Store bin number in I
RDN
1
STO+I        Add 1 to the register
               designated by I
```

6.26 Multi-purpose labels

Many of HP's programmable calculators have two or more keys labeled **A**, **B**, etc., that allow you to execute segments of a program from the keyboard. For example, when you press the **A** key the calculator searches downward from the current position in the program until it finds the first **LBL A**, then it begins execution there.

Sometimes you will find that you need more of these program entry keys than you have on the keyboard. Here is a trick you can use on calculators that allow indirect branching (including the HP-11, 15, and 16). Set up your program like this:

```
LBL A      Entry point for A1, A2, etc.
STO I      The number in X selects which
RDN         of the "A" routines to use.
GTO I
LBL 1      Start of A1 section
...
RTN
LBL 2      Start of A2 section
...
RTN
LBL 3      Start of A3 section
...
RTN
...
...
LBL B      Entry point for B1, B2, etc.
STO I      The number in X selects which
RDN         of the "B" routines to use.
GTO I
```

```
LBL 1        Start of B1 section
...
RTN
LBL 2        Start of B2 section
...
```

and so on. To use this setup, key in the number of the program section you want to execute, then press the appropriate letter key. For example, to execute the A3 section, press

3 **A** .

This technique provides a virtually unlimited number of easy entry points from the keyboard. In fact, you will run out of program memory before you run out of entry points.

Note that you cannot use backward **GTO**'s or **GSB**'s to labels that are re-used. Each backward branch should have its own distinct label.

APPENDIX A

The roots of Reverse Polish Notation

The following text is a summary of an article written by John Kennedy (PPC member 918) and published in the August 1982 PPC Calculator Journal (see Appendix B for information on PPC).

Many people know that RPN stands for Reverse Polish Notation, but few really understand the foundations of this system of notation or know of its significance in the world of calculators and computers. Jan Lucasiewicz was the Polish logician who invented a parenthesis-free notation used to describe logical expressions in the subject generally know as symbolic logic. Because Lucasiewicz's nationality is much easier to remember and pronounce compared to his last name, his system of notation has come to be known as Polish notation.

A description of Lucasiewicz's notation was published in two of his papers in 1929. One of those papers consisted of notes from lectures delivered at Warsaw University in the autumn trimester of the 1928-29 academic year. It is significant that in listing the more important results of his research in mathematical logic, Lucasiewicz chose his parenthesis-free notation as the first item on the list. This idea must have originated in the year 1928 (or earlier), a date that precedes the completion of the first electronic computer by almost 20 years.

Symbolic logic is concerned in part with developing techniques to determine whether or not certain logic sentences follow from certain others. Simple sentences have a truth value within a given context. They can be regarded as the building blocks from which compound sentences can be constructed. In sequential or propositional calculus, simple sentences are combined by using logical connectives. The five standard logical connectives are "and", "or", "not", "if...then...", and "if and only if".

Symbolism is introduced into logic by using single letters of the alphabet to represent sentences and using special symbols to represent the logical connectives. As an example of translation into symbolic form, consider the sentence:

> If George drinks and George does not smoke cigarettes, then George is in good health.

This is a compound sentence made up of three simple sentences. We may let each of the letters p, q, and r denote on of the simple sentences.

> p : George drinks.
>
> q : George smokes cigarettes.
>
> r : George is in good health.

If, in addition, we let the symbol $\sim$ stand for "not", $\Rightarrow$ stand for "if...then...", and $\wedge$ stand for "and", then the above sentence can be written in symbolic form as:

$$(P \wedge \sim q) \Rightarrow r$$

As further illustrations, if we let the letter s denote the sentence:

> s : George should quit his bad habits.

Then the symbolic expression $(p \wedge q) \Rightarrow (\sim r \wedge s)$ would translate into ordinary English as:

> If George drinks and smokes cigarettes, then George is not in good health and he should quit his bad habits.

We have used parentheses in the above two examples of symbolic expressions to indicate proper grouping of sentence variables and logical connectives. The parentheses are needed to eliminate any ambiguity which might be associated with such symbolic forms.

In this sense, the reason for employing parentheses as grouping symbols is identical to the reason for using parentheses in mathematical expressions.

The mathematical expression 2+3*7 may be subject to misinterpretation if one does not agree to, or is not aware of, standard mathematical conventions. If you perform the operations from left to right, you would first add 2 and 3 to get 5, then multiply 5 by 7 to come up with a final answer of 35. Of course you could just as well begin by multiplying 3 and 7 to get 21, then add 2 to that result to get 23 for the final answer. Thus the expression 2+3*7 is ambiguous. One way to remove the ambiguity is to introduce parentheses. If the intended meaning is to add first, you would write (2+3)*7. To specify multiplication first, you would write 2+(3*7).

Although this example is quite simple, it clearly demonstrates the need for parentheses as grouping symbols. In more complicated examples several sets of parentheses may be needed to give an expression its intended meaning. As more parentheses are added, the expression becomes more difficult to read. Strictly speaking, it is not incorrect to add more parentheses than are needed, but it is best to use the minimum number of parentheses needed to make the meaning clear. For this reason certain conventions have been adopted in mathematics.

One of these conventions is that we should perform multiplications and divisions before additions and subtractions. With this idea in mind the expression 2+3*7 is no longer ambiguous. The multiplication is to be performed first. Of course, if you wanted the addition to be performed first, you have to write (2+3)*7.

This convention does not resolve the ambiguity of the simple expression 16/8/2. If you perform the operations left to right the result is 1. But if you perform 8/2 first, the final answer will be 4. Therefore a second convention is added, stating that operations of equal priority are performed left to right.

The calculation procedure is to start at the innermost set of parentheses and work outward, doing multiplication/division before addition/subtraction and calculating left to right at each level of parentheses.

Now let's go back to George. In symbolic logic you can also encounter ambiguity of expressions. This time the variables will denote the following simple sentences:

p : George will play the piano.

q : George will sing.

r : George's sister will sing.

Also, let the symbol v denote the logical connective "or". Then the symbolic expression pvq^r is ambiguous; it can be treated as pv(q^r) or as (pvq)^r. The symbolic expression pv(q^r) translates as:

George will play the piano, or George and his sister will sing.

The expression (pvq)^r translates as:

George will play the piano or sing, and his sister will sing.

The meanings of these two translations are obviously different, since in the second case George's sister is going to sing regardless of what George does.

Just as in mathematics, symbolic logic has

certain conventions that dictate which logical connectives take precedence over others. These conventions also help keep the number of parentheses to a minimum.

Now that you have seen the standard approaches to minimizing the need for parentheses you will be better able to appreciate Lucasiewicz's achievement of devising a parenthesis-free notation. In fact, this notation is free of any kind of grouping!

Lucasiewicz used capital letters to denote the logical connectives:

C :	=>	Conditional	(if...then...)
A :	v	Alternation	(or)
K :	^	Conjunction	(and)
N :	~	Negation	(not)
E :	<=>	Equivalence	(if and only if)

The simple conditional "if p then q", which in standard notation would be denoted by p=>q, is denoted Cpq in Polish notation. The expression p^q becomes Kpq, pvq becomes Apq, and ~p becomes Np.

In this notation, the capital letters which denote the logical connectives act as operators and the lowercase letters act as the operands. The operator is placed to the left of the operands in Polish notation. The order in which the operands follow the operator is important in the case of the operator C. Cpq denotes "if p then q", whereas Cqp denotes "if q then p". Complex symbolic sentences can be formed unambiguously and without parentheses using Polish notation. As Lucasiewicz pointed out, his notation is also very easy to write using a standard typewriter.

The symbolic formula (p^~q)=>r, when written in Polish notation, becomes CKpNqr. This is a well-formed formula (WFF) whose construction can be understood by beginning with the expression in parentheses in the standard notation. There you see $p \wedge \sim q$, which means "p and not q". Nq denotes "not q". When you from the conjunction of p with Nq, you write K to the left of these two terms. Thus KpNq is the antecedent of the above conditional whose consequent is r. To form the complete expression, write both KpNq and r to the right of the letter C. The final form is then CKpNqr.

By similar reasoning, $(p \wedge q) \Rightarrow (\sim r \wedge s)$ becomes CKpqKNrs. The antecedent and consequent of this basic conditional statement are Kpq and KNrs, respectively. The conditional is formed by writing these two terms to the left of the letter C. Now you can easily see why Polish notation does not require parentheses.

Now let's take another look at the performance of George and his sister to see how the symbolic formula $p \vee q \wedge r$ may be rendered unambiguous using Polish notation. The formula $p \vee (q \wedge r)$ becomes ApKqr, while the other variation, $(p \vee q) \wedge r$, becomes KApqr. Note that in the expression ApKqr the connective A applies to p and Kqr, while the connective K applies to q and r. In KApqr, the connective A applies only to p and q, while K applies to Apq and r.

As noted earlier, the reasons for using parentheses in symbolic logic are identical to the reasons for using parentheses in ordinary mathematical notation. In fact, there is a very close relationship between the well-formed formulas (WFFs) in propositional calculus and formulas in mathematics. Every WFF can be translated into a mathematical formula whose only operations are addition, multiplication, and negation. The reverse translation is also possible. By translating WFFs into mathematical formulas we can more clearly see their algebraic character.

The algebra of logic obeys many (but not all) of the laws of arithmetic. When we translate a formula from propositional calculus into a mathematical formula the variables are no longer sentences, but numerical quantities which represent the truth-value of the sentences. Each numerical quantity can take one of two values: 0 or 1. The value 0 denotes FALSE, while 1 denotes TRUE. The logical connectives become the familiar mathematical operations.

For example, logical conjunction translates as multiplication. The WFF $p \wedge q$ becomes $p \cdot q$. Note that if p is TRUE and q is FALSE then the conjunction $p \wedge q$ is FALSE. Substituting 1 for p and 0 for q in the mathematical formula $p \cdot q$ yields $1 \cdot 0 = 0$, which also represents a FALSE result. As a matter of fact, the only time $p \wedge q$ is TRUE is when p and q are both TRUE. Similarly, the only time $p \cdot q$ yields a numerical value 1 is when p and q both take on the value 1.

Alternation is translated into addition. The connective "or" as used in logic always refers to the non-exclusive case. Thus $p \vee q$ means "p or q or possibly both". In order for $p \vee q$ to be TRUE, at least one of p and q must be TRUE. The only time $p \vee q$ is FALSE is when both p and q are FALSE. Note that the only time $p+q=0$ is when both p and q are zero. One slight complication is that we must redefine the + operation slightly so that $1+1=1$. Then, if both p and q are TRUE, the result $p+q$ is still TRUE.

Since negating a TRUE sentence yields a FALSE

one, and vice versa, we must also make the arithmetic definitions $-1=0$ and $-0=1$. Then $\sim p$ translates as $-p$.

Lucasiewicz was an historian of logic. Although Polish notation was originally applied to propositional calculus, Lucasiewicz was well aware of the translation of formulas from symbolic logic into ordinary mathematical notation.

The connection will now become most apparent if we take another look at the above examples of the translation process in terms of Polish notation. Rewriting the above logic formulas in Polish notation and then translating into mathematical notation, we have:

Apq	becomes	+pq
Kpq	becomes	•pq
ApKqr	becomes	+p•qr
AKpNrs	becomes	+•p-rs
AKpqKqNr	becomes	+•pq•q-r
KApqAqr	becomes	•+pq+qr

The reader with sufficient experience will immediately make the connection between the last pseudo-mathematical expressions and how calculations are performed on RPN calculators. Reading the expressions from right to left tells you what quantities are to be entered into the calculation and what operations are to be performed.

Now consider the four analogous and equivalent expressions:

$$p\vee(q\wedge r) \quad p+(q\cdot r) \quad ApKqr \quad +p\cdot qr \ .$$

Reading the fourth expression backwards tells you precisely how to compute the second expression. Following the standard mathematical convention, we should enter r and p into the calculation first, then multiply, then enter p, then add. Reading backwards can be avoided by writing the terms of the expression in **reverse** order.

Eureka! Reverse Polish Notation!

Writing the expression in reverse yields rq·p+, which is the RPN equivalent of the above four notations. The third notation ApKqr is genuine Polish notation as formulated by Lucasiewicz in 1929.

In actual practice mathematical formulas are not written in RPN, but they may be thought of as if they were written that way (especially when the formula is to be evaluated on an RPN calculator. Once the basic principles behind RPN are understood, it is a simple matter to mentally convert from ordinary mathematical notation to RPN while a formula is being read and evaluated. The translation process is as simple for complex formulas as it is for elementary formulas. The big advantage over algebraic logic is that the problem solving is so natural that you do not need to write down the formula at all.

APPENDIX B

Further Reading

1. HP Key Notes is no longer published, but back issues are still available from HP. For price and availability information, write to:

HP Key Notes
1000 N.E. Circle Boulevard
Corvallis, OR 97330 USA

2. The PPC Calculator Journal, published by Personal Programming Center, a users' group organized as a non-profit public benefit California corporation. The Calculator Journal issues from July 1979 (Volume 6, Number 4) to the present cover the HP-41; earlier issues offer helpful hints and programs of more general interest.

To obtain a PPC membership application and a price list for back issues of the Calculator Journal, send $1 to:

PPC Dept. EN
P.O. Box 9599
Fountain Valley, CA 92728-9599 USA

3. The PPC ROM for the HP-41, an 8K custom module for the HP-41, designed by PPC members and manufactured by Hewlett-Packard. The PPC ROM contains 122 programs of general utility, and it comes with a 500-page User's Manual. The program listings, instructions, and line-by-line analysis in the User's Manual are excellent learning tools for aspiring programmers. For price and ordering information, check your calculator dealer or write to PPC at the above address. The PPC ROM User's Manual is also available separately.

4. HP-41 Extended Functions Made Easy, a book by Keith Jarett. 264 pages, plastic spiral bound. A

step-by-step introduction, from the basic concepts of extended memory to explanations and examples of each of the extended functions. The second half of the book presents over 30 utility programs, including a text editor, a mailing list manager, solve, integrate, and more. Check with your calculator dealer or write to:

SYNTHETIX, Dept. EN
P.O. Box 1080
Berkeley, CA 94701-1080 USA

The price per copy is $16.95 plus shipping: $1 (USA, book rate), $2 (USA, United Parcel Service), $3 (USA or Canada, air mail), or $5.55 (elsewhere, air mail). California residents add sales tax. Checks must be payable through a U.S. bank.

5. HP-41 Synthetic Programming Made Easy, a book by Keith Jarett. 192 pages, plastic spiral bound. Introduces the fascinating subject of synthetic programming, encompassing the creation and use of instructions that cannot normally be keyed on the HP-41. Synthetic instructions range from non-standard tones to powerful instructions that access the HP-41's operating system scratch registers. Synthetic capabilities include expanded key assignments and additional display characters. "HP-41 Synthetic Programming Made Easy" contains general utility programs, plus application programs for the Extended Functions and Time modules. The techniques and programs work equally well on the HP-41C, CV, or CX. Includes a plastic Quick Reference Card for Synthetic Programming. Check your dealer or write to SYNTHETIX at the address in item 4. The price and shipping charges are the same as for "HP-41 Extended Functions Made Easy".

6. An Easy Course in Using the HP-12C, a book by Chris Coffin and Ted Wadman. 256 pages, spiral bound. Explains financial computations, why they work, and how to do them on the HP-12C. A self-paced course with examples, self-tests, and handy hints. Check your dealer or write to:

Grapevine Publications, Inc., Dept EN
P.O. Box 118
Corvallis, OR 97339-0118 USA

The price per copy is $17.95 plus shipping, which is $2 (USA), $3.50 (Canada), or $6 (elsewhere). Checks must be payable through a U.S. bank.

7. An Easy Course in Programming the HP-41, a book by Ted Wadman and Chris Coffin. 255 pages, spiral bound. Perfect for beginners. Programmed learning of HP-41 programming! Written by two former HP employees, this book will teach anyone how to program the HP-41. What's more, it's easy and fun. Check your dealer or write to Grapevine (same price and shipping charges as item 6).

8. Calculator Tips and Routines (Especially for the HP-41), a book edited by John Dearing. 130 pages, spiral bound. This book contains many helpful hints, listings of utility programs, and short, useful instruction sequences. This book is available from dealers or directly from:

Corvallis Software, Inc., Dept. EN
P.O. Box 1412
Corvallis OR 97339-1412 USA

The price is $15 within the USA and Canada, $20 elsewhere, airmail prepaid. Checks must be payable through a US bank.

INDEX

ORDER BLANK

	Quantity	Amount
HP-41 Extended Functions Made Easy By Keith Jarett. Introduction to Extended Functions module (built into HP-41CX). Helps you get the most from your Extended Functions. Over 30 powerful utility programs. $16.95 per copy	_____	$ _______
HP-41 Synthetic Programming Made Easy by Keith Jarett. Learn to create and use non-keyable (synthetic) instructions. Multiplies the power and convenience of your HP-41. $16.95 per copy	_____	$ _______
Quick Reference Card (QRC) Indispensable for synthetic programming. Printed on durable plastic. $3.00 each	_____	$ _______
ENTER (Reverse Polish Notation Made Easy) By J.-D. Dodin. Revised and expanded by Keith Jarett to include programming techniques, programs, and tips for owners of HP Series 10 calculators. $12.95 per copy	_____	$ _______
	Subtotal:	$ _______
Sales Tax (California orders only, 6 or 6.5%)		$ _______

Shipping, per book

within USA, book rate (4th class) $1.00
USA 48 states, United Parcel Service $2.00
USA, Canada, air mail $3.00
elsewhere, air mail $5.55

Shipping for QRC plastic cards (any number)

Free with a book order or with a self-addressed, stamped envelope. Otherwise $1.50

Enter shipping total here $ _______

Total enclosed: $ _______

Checks must be payable through a US bank.

Name ______________________________

Address ______________________________

____

City ______________ State ______ Zip ______

Country ______________________________

Mail to:

SYNTHETIX
P.O. Box 1080
Berkeley, CA
94701-1080 USA

ORDER BLANK

	Quantity	Amount
HP-41 Extended Functions Made Easy By Keith Jarett. Introduction to Extended Functions module (built into HP-41CX). Helps you get the most from your Extended Functions. Over 30 powerful utility programs. $16.95 per copy	_____	$ _______
HP-41 Synthetic Programming Made Easy by Keith Jarett. Learn to create and use non-keyable (synthetic) instructions. Multiplies the power and convenience of your HP-41. $16.95 per copy	_____	$ _______
Quick Reference Card (QRC) Indispensable for synthetic programming. Printed on durable plastic. $3.00 each	_____	$ _______
ENTER (Reverse Polish Notation Made Easy) By J.-D. Dodin. Revised and expanded by Keith Jarett to include programming techniques, programs, and tips for owners of HP Series 10 calculators. $12.95 per copy	_____	$ _______
	Subtotal:	$ _______
Sales Tax (California orders only, 6 or 6.5%)		$ _______

Shipping, per book

- within USA, book rate (4th class) $1.00
- USA 48 states, United Parcel Service $2.00
- USA, Canada, air mail $3.00
- elsewhere, air mail $5.55

Shipping for QRC plastic cards (any number)

Free with a book order or with a self-addressed, stamped envelope. Otherwise $1.50

Enter shipping total here $ _______

Total enclosed: $ _______

Checks must be payable through a US bank.

Name ______________________________________

Address ____________________________________

____

City ____________________ State _______ Zip ________

Country ____________________________________

Mail to:

SYNTHETIX
P.O. Box 1080
Berkeley, CA
94701-1080 USA